Publicity still for Ed Wood's *Glen or Glenda?*, my first starring movie role in 1953.

A Fuller Life

HOLLYWOOD, ED WOOD AND ME

The Autobiography of *Dolores Fuller*

with STONE WALLACE AND PHILIP CHAMBERLIN

A Fuller Life
Hollywood, Ed Wood and Me
The Autobiography of Dolores Fuller
©2009 Dolores Fuller

Published in the USA by:
BearManor Media
P.O. Box 71426
Albany, Georgia 31708
www.BearManorMedia.com

ISBN: 1-59393-304-5

with Stone Wallace and Philip Chamberlin

Book design and layout by Valerie Thompson

Ed Wood.   **Johnny Depp as Ed Wood.**

Working on the movie, Johnny Depp called it:

". . . an enlightening experience. I wasn't at all afraid of the idea of working in drag. I considered it an experiment to see what it would be like to wear lots of women's accouterments. And I have to say I have a much deeper respect for women and for transvestites for that matter. I think Ed wore women's clothes because he really loved women and wanted to be that much closer to them. Ed was someone who was not afraid to take chances and did exactly as he wanted to do. He did the best he could with what was available to him and was able to put together images that were surreal with moments of genius, and I think his movies were all his. I hope Ed is remembered as an artist."

— JOHNNY DEPP

(from Disney's Press Release, 1994)

Tim Burton directing *Ed Wood*, a hugely entertaining movie.

Director Tim Burton was instantly drawn to the story of the often misunderstood visionary from the moment he read the treatment.

"I really felt close to him . . . There's something beautiful about somebody who does what they love to do, no matter how misguided and remains optimistic and upbeat against all odds . . . I grew up watching Ed Wood's movies on television. Like everyone else at first, I remember thinking 'Wow, what is this?' But then I began to realize that even though they are bad, they're good. There's something poetic about them. Ed remained true to his work. He didn't let technicalities like visible wires and bad sets distract him from his storytelling. There's a twisted form of integrity to that."

— TIM BURTON

*(Comments made when **Ed Wood** was first released in 1994 by Buena Vista releasing for Disney)*

Johnny Depp as Ed Wood directing in Tim Burton's movie, *Ed Wood.*

A dozen songs sung by Elvis in his Hollywood movies had my lyrics.

Stella Adler soon after her book, *The Art of Acting*, was published.

"I admired Dolores's talent and dedication and I thought she would make a good drama teacher . . ."

— STELLA ADLER

(from Stella Adler's salute to Dolores. See page 126.)

Table of Contents

Foreword
by Stone Wallace

I suppose I was first "introduced" to Dolores Fuller during my college years. This was in 1982 when I was taking a Creative Communications course. This was also around the time that Harry and Michael Medved released their book celebrating the "Worst" in cinematic achievements, "The Golden Turkey Awards." A group of us college buddies were fascinated with the book and we began to hunt down on video a number of the movies listed, our preference leaning towards the older, more obscure titles, which we discovered had been released by a Canadian company called Admit One. Naturally, the films of "Worst Director of All Time" Edward D. Wood, Jr. piqued our curiosity and we decided to skip a few Friday afternoon Sociology classes to gather at one of our homes to view his most infamous pictures: *Glen or Glenda?*, *Bride of the Monster* and the film named by the Medveds "The Worst Movie of All Time," *Plan Nine from Outer Space*.

As a lifelong "horror" movie fan, I reveled in seeing the immortal Bela Lugosi acting out these last villainous screen roles, even as I felt sorrow at seeing how tragic a figure he had become, due to career disillusionment and a medically-induced drug addiction. Still, even at such an advanced stage of artistic decay, in at least one of these films, *Bride of the Monster*, he still possessed his sinister magic.

An added plus for me in viewing these movies was watching for the first time a beautiful young actress named Dolores Fuller. While these Ed Wood films were far beneath the standard of usual Hollywood productions, I saw a dedication and passion in her *Glen or Glenda?* performance that particularly appealed to me. It was evident that even working within the budgetary and story limitations, she was clearly giving her all. While some performers would thumb their noses at appearing in such a film and merely "walk through the part," Dolores truly "acted" her role and provided an intriguing and entertaining characterization. I was impressed, and remain so.

Little did I realize at the time that some 20 years later I would propose to Dolores the idea of assisting her with the writing of her autobiography (many pages of which, unbeknownst to me, she had already penned) and in the process would meet and grow to further admire this extraordinary woman. I spent 8 months as guests of Dolores and her husband, the equally remarkable Dr. Philip Chamberlin, at their lovely home in Las Vegas and say in all sincerity that I have never met two more gracious and generous people. They treated me as "family" during my stay and I regarded them then — as I still do — as "earth angels." Genuinely loving and giving people, never refusing to lend a helping hand to anyone in need. I was both the recipient and was privy to their many acts of kindness, which was unfailingly extended even when they were coping with their own difficulties. I shared good times and bad times with them, but through all of these experiences (including the illness and death of Dolores's beloved son, Darrel) I got to see firsthand the incredible strength, courage and dignity of Dolores Fuller. Equally gratifying was witnessing through fan mail and personal contact the love and devotion expressed by her many fans, sentiments that Dolores always reciprocated with genuine appreciation.

As I set about working with Dolores and Philip on the book, I came to learn much about the "other" professional life of Dolores Fuller, one still heavily rooted in the entertainment field, and many of these accomplishments were admittedly unknown to me. These stories, told in Dolores's own words, are not only fascinating, but stand as an indictment against recent hurtful criticism aimed at Dolores Fuller's talents.

It really began when Tim Burton's biopic of 1950's film director Ed Wood was released in October, 1994. Disney's publicity department tried to get Johnny Depp, the star of **Ed Wood**, to make the usual promotional rounds to call attention to the film's release. Depp's star was rapidly rising at the time, but unfortunately he was not available, so Disney tapped Sarah Jessica Parker for the job — not realizing that Parker would seize the opportunity to call attention to herself rather than serve the best interests of the movie. Whether in print or on television, the one question always asked of her was "How did you prepare for the role of Dolores Fuller?" Parker had a stock response: "It doesn't take much preparation to play the world's worst actress." Translation: "I didn't prepare."

It is unlikely there has ever been a more crude, unfair assessment made of a fellow actor's talents, particularly rendered by one who based her opinion not on careful research of her subject, but on a completely unjustified inference from the Medveds' labeling of Eddie who certainly was *not* Hollywood's worst director, as both Tim Burton and Johnny Depp have made clear in their statements. Had Parker taken time to do her homework, she may have been surprised to discover that Dolores Fuller's acting career was not limited to starring in such low-budget productions as **Glen or Glenda?** (1953) or her bit in **Bride of the Monster** (1955), which Burton regarded highly enough to quote precisely in his movie with scenes that carefully copied footage originally shot by Ed Wood. Dolores had appeared in several "A"-list pictures featuring top stars and directors. She also later studied under the legendary Stella Adler at the renowned Actor's Studio, and delivered smash performances as Cherie and Lotus Blossom in summer stock productions of **Bus Stop** and **The Teahouse of the August Moon**, respectively.

Nor was acting her only accomplishment. Always looking to expand her horizons, Dolores next embarked on a highly successful songwriting career, creating memorable lyrics for Nat King Cole, Peggy Lee and, especially, Elvis Presley, whose rendition of Dolores's "Rock-a-Hula Baby" for the 1961 hit **Blue Hawaii** remains a favorite of many Elvis fans to this day.

Dolores had a knack for discovering and promoting talent, and among her major finds were Johnny Rivers, Ronnie Fuller and Tanya Tucker. Dolores admits that out of her many professional endeavors she received the most satisfaction from nurturing and assisting promising singers and artists as shown in the hour-long documentary on her life, **Diamonds in the Rough**, which appeared on German Television in 1997 and subsequently was repeated.

Dolores remains a busy optimist with a full agenda, including frequent appearances at film festivals and autograph collector shows throughout the country. During the past several years she has worked on a stage musical together with talented songsmith Scott Martin which centers around certain events in her life with Edward D. Wood (hopefully for Broadway) tentatively titled *Ed Wood . . . But I Wouldn't*. Portions of this book will give the reader an idea of the period covered in the stage show.

Dolores has certainly enjoyed the "romance of living," with its many ups and downs. Hence this book's title: *A Fuller Life*. It certainly has been — and is.

Preface & Acknowledgements
"... a story must be told!"

(Ed Wood's words, powerfully delivered by Bela Lugosi in *Glen or Glenda?*, have existential truth that echoes down the corridors of time. Well, at least they have been echoing down my corridor for the past ten years, stimulated largely by Tim Burton's film, *Ed Wood*, hence this book):

There are many other reasons why I decided to write my autobiography, not the least of which is the number of requests I receive from my fans. Over the past ten years, my dear husband, Philip Chamberlin, and I have been frequent guests at film festivals, autograph and collector shows and, very often, I have been asked when I might be coming out with a book about my life. With Philip's help, I actually began a book that I hoped would set the record straight. Some years ago, after the movie, *Ed Wood*, was released, I received a letter from Wade Williams who owns the rights to Ed Wood's first feature film, *Glen or Glenda?*, proposing that I write a stage musical based on the film. This proposal had an intoxicating appeal. I had always wanted to write a Broadway show and, after all, a key portion of that movie was autobiographical — Ed Wood's struggle with himself to decide whether or not to tell me about his compulsion to cross dress. He feared that I might not marry him if he told me. I began to exercise Wade's commission and wrote a key song, "A New Kind Of Man." Wade really didn't care for it and I had to re-think my approach. Through my professional organization in New York, ASCAP (American Society of Composers Authors and Publishers), I found my way to a co-writer who had an impressive accomplishment in writing stage musicals. Additionally, I came to feel that the full story of Eddie and Dolores was a better basis for a stage show than **Glen or Glenda?** and, after working with my new co-writer, Scott Martin, for a while, I realized that an autobiography should come first.

While the Tim Burton movie was wonderfully entertaining, it was not entirely factual (after all, it was never intended as a documentary). And, though Johnny Depp gave a typically outstanding performance that I enjoyed immensely, the script did not allow him to portray the real Eddie. Audiences whose only knowledge of Eddie was through the Burton film — and perhaps showings of Eddie's own pictures — were not given a complete or an accurate view of the Edward D. Wood I knew and loved. That, I felt, should be corrected and in so doing, I hope to touch on parts of the film and television world and the wider world I knew from the early 1930's to the present.

Beginning even before the Medved brothers wrote their books "celebrating" the worst in filmmaking, a cult started growing around Eddie, culminating with the publication of a meticulously researched book by Rudolph Grey, "Nightmare of Ecstasy: The Life and Art of Edward D. Wood, Jr.," which corresponded with many facts and non-facts in the script that Tim Burton decided to use for his picture. Rudolph conducted dozens of interviews over the ten year period that it took for him to write his book and he never tried to do the impossible, which was to distinguish fact from rumor, opinion and hearsay. This gave his work a "Citizen Kane" kind of richness that I loved. But it left the door open for the script-writers to ignore facts that didn't suit their approach. Also, there is no doubt in my mind that the script Burton used was heavily influenced by the Medveds, principally owing to a perceived potential for humor. But, highly entertaining though it was, **Ed Wood** did not result in the kind of recognition Eddie would have fully appreciated, or deserved. Too much attention was focused on Eddie's limited skills as a moviemaker and, particularly, on his transvestism. These have been over-emphasized, leaving people with an unflattering, eccentric image of a man possessed of many positive qualities. The Eddie I knew — and I probably knew him better than anybody else — was a kind, considerate and charming man, a loyal friend to everyone with whom he worked, a superlative dancer whose chief connection with the Johnny Depp/Tim Burton interpretation was his passion for making movies.

Also, I felt that I had not been treated fairly or accurately in my onscreen characterization by Sarah Jessica Parker. She simply never bothered to call me to talk about the role, or do any other research that might have led to a more truthful interpretation of my character in **Ed Wood**. The other lead actresses in the picture, Patricia Arquette and Lisa Marie, made it a point to meet with the women they portrayed, Kathy Wood and Maila Nurmi (Vampira) respectively, but not Parker. And so, when the film came out and her performance was generally panned (much of it had actually been left on the cutting room floor), she came back defensively, the only way she could think up, and started telling interviewers that it was not much of a challenge to be playing the "worst actress ever in the history of film." This, I think, hurt the movie because the more she went around bad-mouthing me, the less business the picture did.

Also, when Tanya Tucker's biography came out in 1997, I was terribly hurt by the fact that she used every opportunity to justify the illegal, insensitive and self-serving action of her father in violating his contract with me as her personal manager once I got Tanya a contract with Columbia Records that launched her career. She begrudged me any credit and signed her name to an account that was full of mistakes and uncharitable comment. The truth needs to be served. It is my intention to document the real story in this book for those who care about accuracy. The book that Philip and I began ten years ago was never finished, though several chapters were written and are incorporated here. When Canadian writer Stone Wallace contacted me in mid-2004 expressing BearManor Media's interest in publishing my autobiography, we saw the perfect opportunity to work with Stone, flesh out what I had written, clear up the rumors and tell the complete story — as someone who lived it.

I would be remiss if I did not acknowledge other important help given me by many whom I called on over the years in order to get the facts straight and for aid in what for me has been the daunting task of completing a book. Especially, I am grateful to Arne Folkedal for his photographic expertise in scanning photos for this book and, in the process, helping in a great variety of ways. Arne set up the photographic department at the Academy of Motion Picture Arts and Sciences for my husband in 1972. His intelligence and far-ranging competence in a number of fields were all brought to bear here on my behalf. Howard Green at Disney, not only did a superbly professional job in promoting Tim Burton's movie despite the handicap of dealing with Michael D. Eisner's order to dump *Ed Wood* into wide release — when it should have been given leisurely special handling — he sent my husband and me press materials of vital importance to this book. Dear friends, Cliffie Stone, Brett Thompson, Bob Evans and Eric Caiden went far beyond the call of duty in many special ways. And dear Vicky Fletcher has grown even more in my affection with her time and her attention to details that I never could remember by myself. I must also thank National Artists Foundation, Wade Williams, Scott Martin, Doug Sellars, Cindy Robin, Ray and Sharon Courts, Buddy Barnett, Cinema Collectors, Eric Caidin, Hollywood Book and Poster, Joe Strafford, Elena DaVinci, Ric and Micky Hardman, Murray and Rhoda Glass, the Academy of Motion Picture Arts and Sciences, Megan Heryet, Nick E. Poulakis, Jay Ramsey, Barbara Bogar, Gloria Pall, Carlo Roncancio and, of course, Stone Wallace. With Stone's extraordinary skill as midwife to my memory, old recollections were reborn and cry out to be told. So, with thanks to all my fans who have requested it over the years and for others who may be interested, this is my story.

— DOLORES FULLER
LAS VEGAS, NEVADA
AUGUST, 2008

My Early Years
Chapter One

From my earliest years, my Mother taught me that what counts most lies deep within a person, it's not what you see on the surface. While both my Mother and Grandmother took great pains to brush my long blonde curls around their fingers and dress me like a little doll, they took even greater care to teach me that the most important aim in life is to be the best person I could possibly be. To share with others, to not be selfish, to live by the Golden Rule: Do unto others as you would have others do unto you. But one can give a great deal to help others without regard to the need to protect one's self at the same time. There are always opportunists ready to take advantage of the unwary with consequent heartache. I've learned this the hard way. *"Be the best person you can be,"* they said.

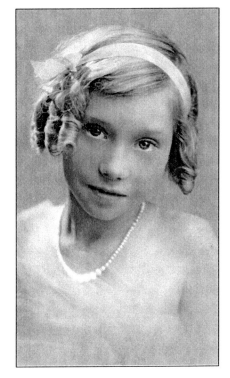

Yes. What's inside *is* most important, but having physical beauty certainly is a help! For better or worse, the world values appearances highly and nowhere is this truer than in Hollywood. The lure of movie stardom draws attractive girls to Southern

California by the thousands. Many of these hopefuls lack brain power, common sense or the slightest trace of talent. Most of these unfortunate girls fall by the wayside, frequently drifting into dire poverty or prostitution. Some take refuge in marriage when they tire of making the rounds of Hollywood's casting couches. Others quickly waken to reality and seek "regular" employment. And . . . a few — a *very* few — succeed in what is, without a doubt, one of the most highly competitive endeavors on earth. To "make it" in the movie business, a girl has to have beauty, talent, dedication . . . and, most especially, intelligence. This intelligence doesn't necessarily have to be exclusive to the actress; it can be shared by the proper representation of a manager or an agent. Even Marilyn Monroe had Johnny Hyde, her devoted agent, who sadly died of a broken heart after working tirelessly to get her started.

But one thing is certain: beauty, brains, intelligence and talent alone are not enough. A driving ambition to "be somebody" through achievement — to make life count, is probably the key necessity. The supreme Allied Commander in World War I, General Foch, had a slogan that applies to success in life: "action and tenacity above all." Both are essential in the pursuit of one's dreams.

It always seemed to me that I had enough of both the physical attributes and gray matter to enjoy a successful career in Hollywood through acting, modeling, singing and dancing. I was blessed by genes and Mother Nature with good bone structure, great legs, erect 5'5" posture, a high bust of 34 DD cup, a 25-inch waist and 36-inch hips. My figure was curvy, firm and athletic because I had been on the track and swimming teams in high school, and had taken dancing lessons from the time I was twelve years old. I learned to excel in swimming as a result of working at the El Monte, California Municipal Pool and being coached by their top instructor. Being chosen for the high school swimming team came as a natural progression. During my early teen years I was something of a tomboy and did some foolish things out of my competitive spirit. I wish I could impress on kids today how important it is to avoid the kinds of competition that might result in physical injury, and to form healthy habits such as drinking lots of pure water every day and eating more vegetables and fish. It is so important to avoid junk food and, especially, deep fried food of all kinds. I don't mean to preach, but one's health is the most precious of assets.

My eyes are deep blue and my cheekbones are high. I have been told that, as the years have gone by, my face has developed more character. Certainly I have now developed more wrinkles! I've been described as hard working, ambitious, resourceful, thoughtful and creative to the point of being able to make something out of nothing. But these qualities have, on occasion, been undercut by being too naïve and trusting of people. I've been hurt many times over the years, emotionally and financially. But we live in a different world today than when I began my career over fifty years ago. It's fair to say that people were not stung as often in those long-ago days. Trust was not a foolish virtue, and your word or a handshake was your bond, in many instances more binding than a contract is today. I don't wish to leave you with the impression that I have become jaded — just more cautious. It's still possible to trust people today and not have to kick yourself afterward, but the odds, I believe, are greater now than they used to be that you will be skinned by those you think you can trust.

I was born in South Bend, Indiana to Leonora Dahms and Eugene Eble but was deprived by my Hungarian grandmother, Valeria Kertesz Dahms (born in 1881), of the chance for a "normal" upbringing. Her maiden name, Kertesz, is exactly the same as the original Hungarian name of director Michael Curtiz. I have never learned if they were related, but the possibility is provocative. Nevertheless, my grandmother's story is fascinating far beyond the way it influenced my life. She was a strong-willed, classic Magyar beauty, full breasted with a spectacular 20-inch waist.

Her long, thick reddish-brown hair cascaded down to her waist in curls with little curls on each side of her forehead and the crown of her head piled high with waves. Valeria was smart, well educated and with an unusual command of language. She had an inner strength that made everyone know that she could be in charge. Her innate femininity made her very sexy which came through when she was on stage or when she was around someone she liked. Her enchanting dark green eyes would melt any resistance. I always wondered what would prompt a young girl from a high

Grandma Valeria Kertesz

class, well-to-do family to just pick up and leave her homeland, forsaking friends and all that was familiar, abandoning a promising career that was just beginning to bring her notice for her lovely contralto voice, trained in the Budapest Conservatory of Music and performing in a Budapest opera company. No doubt she was adventurous but she once told me that there was a man who made her some promises. "If you ever get to America, just look me up. I'll make you a star in New York at the Metropolitan Opera!" She and a girl friend stowed away in a ship sailing for America. The help that was promised did not materialize. The "agent-manager" wanted more than the virtuous, seventeen-year-old was willing to give.

Utilizing Hungarian connections, she got a live-in job to support herself in the German-Hungarian neighborhood of west Chicago. Valeria was a talented seamstress who had been taught to sew — part of her upbringing — as were so many European women in those late nineteenth-century days. Here she met August Dahms, who had established himself in the tool and die field and who only wanted Valerie for his wife. It was the classic American split between the arts in which women

August and Valeria Dahms with my mother, Leonora Dahms Eble (about 1909).

take a keen interest and the sciences, in those days usually dominated by men. Sometimes opposites *do* attract. They were married on January 7,1899 and "Gus" provided a nice home that was soon filled with fine furniture, crystal and china.

My mother, Leonora, was born to Valerie and Gus in 1902 about three years after their marriage and Grandma raised her on a satin pillow. Grandma was an accomplished pianist and taught my mother to play and sing and to read extensively, to be a fine lady and not be concerned with menial work. Grandma expected Leonora to marry an up-scale, wealthy man and play hostess to an easy life. When Leonora walked into a room and smiled, it was like a ray of sunshine. Today, you might describe her figure as needing a double DD cup brassier. She was big-busted and had a perfectly proportioned body, but was very petite — only five foot, two. She had great legs that were emphasized by the "flapper" dresses that were the fashion of the 1920's era and she loved to dance the Charleston. When she met Eugene Eble, he was working for the Detroit Railway Company. Later, he ran the company as its

My mother, Leonora Dahms Eble in 1905 and in 1921 — from a satin pillow to a closet full of sobs.

president before he retired on a comfortable pension. One warm summer day in June, Eugene took Leonora on a picnic. They rented a rowboat and paddled out on the lake. When he looked into her beautiful green eyes and she looked into his expressive, tender blue eyes, they were overwhelmed by their love and desire for each other and their passion took over. They found a remote spot in the surrounding woods where Leonora surrendered her virtue, as they say, but that's how I came into the world. I was a "love child," so maybe that's why I've always wanted to give love to others.

There was a timely Catholic wedding and, of course, Grandma was fit to be tied. She wanted so much more for her daughter, but she didn't give Gene a chance to prove himself. My father bought a fine three-bedroom home on Lake Michigan on the north side of Chicago for their starter home. The depression was not yet under way, but some of Gene's buddies were out of work and his brother, Bill, was in need of help. Frank Gardener and Bill moved in with

Gene and Leonora. Mother was very pregnant with me and had never really worked in her life. She weighed less than a hundred pounds, soaking wet. The responsibility of cooking, sewing, cleaning house and washing for three men was more than she could handle, but she was willing to try. As I was to learn, she had come home from shopping for groceries carrying two heavy bags full of supplies to cook dinner for the gang. Then she was down in the basement doing laundry when she passed out cold on the cement floor. At that precise moment, Grandma happened to come for a visit from South Bend, Indiana where she and Gus had made their home. Grandma took over. No way was anyone — not even a husband — going to make a workhorse out of her daughter and endanger her losing her baby. She bundled Mother into the car and took her home to South Bend to care for her. Grandma was furious with Eugene who wrote to Mother every day. Grandma intercepted the letters and never told Mother about them, meanwhile arranging for an annulment of the marriage. Mother was broken hearted and spent a lot of time crying during the balance of the pregnancy. Eugene took his only day off and made the trip to South Bend to try and see Leonora. Grandma had such control over Mother that she was able to hide her in a closet and forbid her to come out until told to do so. After many additional trips and never once being able to see Mother or even to be allowed into Grandma's house, Gene gave up until after I was born. He then demanded to see the baby. Grandma finally had to yield to Gene's increasingly strong insistence, although she would only let him into the screened porch and again forbid Mother to come out while he was there. As Gene laughingly later told me, when he held me for the first time, I wet on him. Grandma never knew the sadness she caused me by her selfish actions in breaking up my parents. How different my life would have been with my own father to love and care for me and give me a model for my later choices of men. But Grandma was a strong lady and controlled the situation. She led Gene to believe that Mother wanted nothing more to do with him. Meanwhile, Mother sobbed in the closet. As I grew older, I did a lot of that myself — crying for my daddy. All Mother told me was that she loved my daddy but that he had broken her heart. My Father was a Catholic who did not believe in divorce. When I found him years later, he told me that he had only one marriage, the one to my Mother. Gene loved music and often went to a little night club where he could listen and try to forget and ease the hurt. "Mimi" was a pretty little French girl who played piano and had her own band. She came on to Gene like gang busters because he was handsome, six feet two and had a good, steady position. She easily seduced him and made him forget some of the hurt he felt in losing Leonora. Gene didn't have much spare time because he worked long hours — another way of escaping his private pain. Also, the distance between Chicago and South Bend made it hard to pursue Mother, especially when Mimi was pursuing him. Mother had been so unhappy during this period that she named me Dolores, which means sadness, sorrows or pains in Spanish. A few years later, Mother took to saying she had named me after the incandescently beautiful Dolores del Rio — which couldn't have been true because that dazzling Mexican beauty did not light up movie screens until the mid-1920's, a few years *after* I was born on March 10, 1923. However, I have always been flattered by the allegation and my vanity led me to go along with the myth.

My grandmother doted on me and raised me until I was five years old while Mother, who was well educated and very well read, went to business school to learn short-hand, typing and courses that would quality her as a legal stenographer. She made an excellent appearance and it didn't take her long to land a good job with a leading law firm. After a time the Jewish attorney that she worked for fell in love with her and asked her to marry him. Mother refused because she was still hurting from her divorce that Grandma had arranged. However, the attorney persuaded her to go ahead with the divorce and to get child support.

Grandma dressed me like a little princess and, until that unhappy day when I had to leave and go with my mother and her new husband, I truly believed that I actually was a princess. As a child, I always had the same dream over and over of being able to just raise above all the other children that I was playing with and fly. I would fly above them in a room or fly around outside and they would try to fly and could not. I was so spoiled and made to think that I was very special, so it was hard for my new step-father to handle me. I remember Grandmother's house as a place to be proud of.

It was in a nice neighborhood and I could play next door with the children of a very wealthy family in the automotive field. We would ride our tricycles together on the grounds of their estate. Being with Grandma was to feel the warmth of her love. She taught me songs and would sing to me with her marvelous voice, but she loved me and spoiled me to a point that, when I had to leave her, I became so unhappy that I would cry myself to sleep at night, longing to be back with her and praying for my own daddy to find me. When I would see other little girls being loved and sitting on their daddy's lap, I would get a lump in my throat. When a little girl would show off a new dress to her daddy and whirl around and get the father's love that I was missing, it would hurt me to the point of tears. I spent a lot of my childhood crying because I just didn't want to be with my Mother's new husband who really didn't love me and was always finding a reason to spank me. I think he resented the additional responsibility. My Mother really did love me but lacked the "take charge" personality of Grandma. She was caught in between Jack who

As a child, I loved being spoiled by my Grandma. She even got me a pony.

I dearly loved my sister, Sylvia. It was as if my beloved Peaches had come to life. Laurence Huett (right), a neighbor, helped me teach her to walk.

was trying to discipline me — admittedly a tough task considering how Grandma trained me to be a princess — and the need to protect me from Jack's strap. I was fast and would run around the dining room table as he pursued me with his strap and Mother screaming for him to stop. I just wanted to be back in Grandma's safe arms where I had dolls like "Peaches" who was as big as I was. Oh! How I cried and carried on when Mother and Jack took me with them and I couldn't take Peaches with me. In fairness to Jack, I must say that his treatment of me improved a great deal after my half-sister, Sylvia Glidewell, was born and I loved her and cared for her as if Peaches had come to life. Indeed, I lavished care and attention on her with every little nuance my Grandma had instilled in me.

My recollections of Grandfather Dahms, of German-Swiss decent, are highly favorable. He was a down-to-earth, old-world gentleman and took me for long walks which I greatly enjoyed. Meanwhile Grandma took a position as governess with an aristocratic family in South Bend, where she fit in well. Sad to say, she looked down on my Grandfather and seemed to feel that she had "married beneath her station." Nevertheless, my Grandfather remained devoted to her and was always available to help in any way possible and to care for Grandmother "beyond the call of duty," as the saying goes. About 1927, Grandma suffered from a stroke that left her blind, but still managed quite well despite the handicap by exercising her extraordinary memory for the precise location of almost every item in the household. Even on the basement shelves, she was so organized she could put her hands on any of the canned goods she wished. She was still able to cook, wash and perform most household chores.

My mother had obtained a good position as a legal secretary for an attorney in South Bend and, about 1928, married Jack Glidewell, a handsome specialist in color printing. Then the great depression of 1929 hit and Jack lost his job, as did so many able-bodied Americans. To make ends meet, Jack and my mother took to the road in his little pick-up truck and sold auto parts to gasoline stations across the country. They took me along because Mother wanted me with her and, also, she knew that I couldn't tolerate the cold Indiana winters. However, one acute discomfort was merely

Vagabond days: our home-on-wheels beginning about 1929. I was car-sick much of the time.

substituted for another because, during those tender years, I often got car-sick. This and the need for schooling led my parents to place me in a Catholic orphanage/school near San Francisco. The Sisters were strict so, at an early age, I acquired discipline. Sweet were the uses of adversity. The sisters believed that each individual student should be assigned a "useful" activity, so I soon found myself cleaning and waxing the dining room floor. I recall vividly the school's wonderful summer camp in the mountains where I learned to swim. There, one evening by the magical light of a campfire, I volunteered to be hypnotized and, according to peer reports, got up, sang, danced and entertained.

These reports surprised me but I think they must have remained buried in my mind until they were unearthed some years later by exposure to Hollywood. Otherwise, I was not happy with the sisters because I missed my Mother and remember crying myself to sleep on more than one occasion. When I graduated from the sixth grade in 1933, my parents again took me on the road, although it was a brief one to Southern California where they intended to settle in El Monte, then a quiet suburb only ten miles east of downtown Los Angeles.

As President of the 4-H Club, I got an all-expenses paid trip to Washington.

Always enterprising and able to find ways of supporting his family, Jack put a down payment on a fine home and, until we could move in, we stayed at a motel that Frank Capra happened to pick for filming the "walls of Jericho" sequence of *It Happened One Night* that became a key event in my life, although I didn't know it at the time. More about that later in my story.

I was enrolled in an El Monte grammar school to finish my elementary grades six, seven and eight (now called "middle school"), and plunged into the life of the community. I joined the grade school orchestra and played steel guitar. The following year, I joined the 4-H Club that promotes high ideals of civic responsibility and training for community leadership (my **H**ead to clearer thinking, my **H**eart to greater loyalty, my **H**ands to larger service, my **H**ealth to better living for my Club, my community, and my country). I

My sister, Sylvia, and I became the closest of friends living in El Monte.

was guided into and through the 4-H Club years by my dear mother and I have always felt that it played a vitally important part in my life development. I followed the 4-H path throughout high school, learning to sew, cook and can. I was extremely proud of being elected President of my Club in my senior year. As a consequence, I was treated to a three-day stay in Washington, D.C., an all-expenses paid trip where I and two girls from other parts of the country were given a guided tour through the White House and to the Lincoln Memorial and Washington Monument. Such stand-out experiences in my youth were highly educational.

When I was 12 years old, I desperately wanted to take dancing lessons, but there just wasn't enough money. Why? Because the monthly child support money which the court had ordered my father to pay until I was eighteen reached me only twice in all those

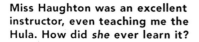

Miss Haughton was an excellent instructor, even teaching me the Hula. How did *she* ever learn it?

Swimming has been my life-long love as the best exercise.

years. My father dutifully gave it to his wife, Mimi, to mail to me, but she deceived him and kept it for herself. Later, she deceived him with another man, resulting in a divorce. I just had to find a way to get those dance lessons. A friend of mine who came from a wealthy family had enrolled in dance classes at the Lillian Haughton School of Dance in El Monte and I used to go with her to watch. Then I would go home and practice what the teacher had taught that session. After some months, I worked up enough nerve to approach Miss Haughton and ask if I could audition for her. I couldn't afford proper ballet toe-shoes, so I concocted my own. I stuffed the toes of my slippers with cotton and sewed long ribbons onto the slippers that I tied around my ankles — then performed an impromptu ballet number based on what I had learned from watching the class. Miss Haughton was horrified at my potentially dangerous toe shoes but was impressed with what I had accomplished on my own and my lust for learning to dance. I passed the audition but there was still the matter of tuition. Boldly, I asked if I could work out a barter arrangement. To my delight, she agreed. In exchange for

I loved to twirl my baton and lead the parade as Head Majorette at El Monte High School!

dance lessons, I would clean the floor after class, sprinkling sawdust over the hardwood floor and sweep it forward with a push broom to remove all the dust. But I had my pride. I didn't want any of the other students to know of this arrangement. She agreed and I began my training with total dedication, excelling at tap, ballet and acrobatics. Miss Haughton even taught me the Hawaiian hula and kept her end of the bargain we had struck. The terms of my lessons were never mentioned to anyone.

My life has always been a whirlwind of activity, and I can't imagine it any other way. I got an after-school job as a locker-girl at the local swimming pool and took swimming lessons from the pool life guard. Later at El Monte High School, I took baton twirling lessons from a husky but talented, dark-haired girl who had won the National Championship. The skills I learned from her plus my experience in dance gave me an edge and led to my being chosen as the Head Majorette at El Monte High School. Using my sewing skills developed in the 4-H Club, I made my own majorette costume.

My school colors were blue and white, so I made a one-piece jump suit with white satin slacks and a figure-flattering top of royal blue. We won the national championship and participated in the

Rose Parade. Tossing the baton high, doing cartwheels down the parade streets and lifting my legs high in the marching band may have helped develop my strong, healthy body. I participated in all sports, with a particular love for running track, swimming and dance. But I suppose my greatest passion was music. One of the most treasured memories of my childhood was that of my Mother playing the piano and singing. The two of us often sat at our old upright piano, singing duets. We couldn't afford piano lessons for me, but I invariably hear the melody in my head when I write a song and I sing the lyrics as I write. I've always regretted not being able to attend the Julliard School of Music. How much further I might have been able to progress at a younger age in the field of my dreams!

Perhaps I was genetically predisposed in my ambition to get into show business, since my second cousin on my father's side of the family was the legendary Broadway star, Lillian Russell, the "Belle of the Ninety's." I was to be her only living female relative to follow her into show business. One of the first signs of my show biz inclination was the impulse to try out for a minor part in a stage play during my senior year in high school. Much to my surprise, I was given the lead! I worked hard on my role and enjoyed it. But the more prosaic fact is that my career got launched in a very large part by the need to find a way out of a stultifying, unhappy marriage. Earlier in my life I might have been better off just staying single, as I was in New York during the eight years that I wrote songs for Elvis Presley. But life is a series of choices, and making what one hopes is the right decision can be difficult when one lacks the wisdom that comes with maturity. Even with maturity, choices can be difficult. During my last two years of high school, age fifteen and a half to seventeen, I had done modeling work. My first attempts at modeling were rebuffed because I had no significant experience and no recognized training. Always determined to find a way to do what I wished, I went to an agency that supplied models for "Market Week," only to be informed that they could not so much as supply me with an interview. Never one to take "no" for an answer, I went to Market Week at the Biltmore in Los Angeles on my own and looked around. I found a line of clothes that I thought would look good on me and approached the lady who managed the store, asking to try on something that I especially liked. When the lady complimented me, I told her that what I would really like would be to model her line of clothes for the rest of the week. Of course she asked if I had any experience and I tweaked the truth a wee bit by assuring her that I was a regular model for a "high class establishment in El Monte." It was true that I was a regular model, except that El Monte had no venues that could by any stretch of the imagination be called high class. I was hired, worked hard during Market Week and, by the second or third day, the manager left the store to me during lunch breaks and other occasions when she had to attend meetings. I made sales in her absence and wrote up the orders. When Market Week was over, the manager agreed to call me "Assistant Manager" on any subsequent referrals. This experience impressed other companies when I auditioned for modeling work and soon I was very busy earning money during my Junior and Senior years.

But a promising start was nipped in the bud by bad judgment on my part in allowing a very attractive but self-assertive boy to dominate me. I had grown up without a father's guidance because my mother and father were divorced when I was a mere infant. I was raised until I was five years old by my Hungarian grandparents while my Mother worked for an attorney as a legal stenographer. At seventeen I was very naïve and unsure of myself with the opposite sex. Without really understanding how it happened (does anyone at that age ever understand how things happen?), I found myself dating a young high school graduate. We met by chance, as is so often the case. At age sixteen I was working part-time during the summer of 1939 at a drive-in restaurant. The owner, always alert for ways to attract business, had me stand out front wearing my majorette costume and twirl my marching-band baton when not serving customers. One afternoon I was twirling away when Don Fuller drove past. It was almost exactly like the scene in *It Happened One Night* when Claudette Colbert showed Clark Gable how to hitch a ride. Don slammed on his brakes, spun around, came back and engaged me in conversation. Don was handsome, sexy, two years older than me and macho-sure of himself. We dated for nearly a year when the Westwood Knitting Mills, who employed me as their sweater girl, modeling and photographing their new line each

During my Senior year in High School, I was sponsored in the Miss America Contest.

season, sponsored me in the Miss America Contest. The El Monte Chapter of the American Legion was my co-sponsor. My participation in the early stages of the contest occurred just before my high school graduation in 1940. Since I loved to sew and couldn't find a bathing suit that I thought was special enough for the contest, I decided to make my own. I found a leopard-spotted fabric that seemed just right and created my own two-piece bathing suit to show off my figure. I suppose my abbreviated costume was rather daring for that pre-war, pre-bikini period because it attracted a lot of favorable comment from the men who organized the Long Beach, California preliminary phase of the competition and I was encouraged to think that there might be a chance for me to get to the finals of the contest. But this opportunity was suddenly cut short at the very moment that I was proudly strutting in front of the judges, reveling in their attention. As I reached the end of the runway, Don materialized out of the crowd, took me by the hand and walked me down the stage steps and away with the stunning command: "Come on, we're getting married." I was flattered instead of realizing what this episode revealed about his possessive character. It seemed to me later that he just couldn't stand having all those men see so much of my body exposed by my bathing suit. But, at the time, my hormones propelled me to agree to his precipitously proposed wedding date, the Sunday after graduation, which was less than a month away! I was much too young, my own physical needs were too strong, and I failed to see the fatal pattern. Don expected his wife to be his private property, exclusively serving his personal wishes. So, in June of 1940. Don and I were married in the First Presbyterian Church of El Monte, California with my beloved sister, Sylvia, as a junior bridesmaid.

After a honeymoon in Mexico, we went to live with Don's parents in a home at the edge of an orange grove in San Dimas. For a while, the marriage seemed idyllic. Before two years had passed, World War II had begun. Don was in training as an army air corps pilot and I had a good job with Douglas Aircraft in Santa Monica, California, towing airplanes behind my jeep from the assembly line to the airport runway. When Don finished training, he was assigned to teach flying at White Sands, New Mexico and I was happy in a small apartment, cooking on a two-burner hot plate and playing

My step-father, Jack Glidewell, was an expert fisherman, but no good as a parent.

cards at the officers' club with other wives. Looking back, I can see that I was complacently marking time until the war ended in August of 1945. Then we returned to San Dimas where Don built a home on a ten-acre hill owned by his parents overlooking Puddingstone Lake.

Jack Glidewell had died so I pitched in and drove each day to my mother's home in El Monte where I worked in the old garage/barn making "Blue Devil" fishing leaders which Jack had invented and was the reason that he always came back from the tuna grounds off the coast between San Diego and Ensenada, Mexico with the biggest and best catch. I wove seven strands of transparent leader on the little machine that Jack devised and supplied the thriving Blue Devil business until mother re-married in 1947. A big Armenian

With husband, Donald K. Fuller, when he was a flight instructor during World War II.

named William Hambasian had been courting her. "Bill" was a good dancer and often drove my mother places she needed to go because mother didn't drive. Bill had a rudimentary knowledge of the real estate business in aspects other than sales and seemed to have had his eye on the Blue Devil income. As soon became evident, he had no talent for fishing leader sales either, so the Blue Devil business became dormant and reels of leader and hooks lay neglected in the barn for thirty years, as did Bill's "office" in the back. During this period, I did my best to be the wife Don wanted me to be, but he continually hurt my feelings by not being supportive of my need for self-expression. Whenever I would feel like singing (and I still enjoy on occasion "bursting into song"), Don would tell me, "You can't sing. You're a monotone." If I tried to write a song, he would blast up the volume on the radio, sadistically destroying my concentration. He incessantly tried to break my spirit rather than encourage me. Don would dish out the sarcasm, laugh at my early efforts to write songs and assure me that I was wasting my time.

I continued to get work modeling clothes after WWII.

Perhaps it was my fault for allowing him to intimidate me. Today, of course, I would stand up for my right to express myself. But back then I didn't seem able to cope with the way he constantly belittled any creative effort I made to express myself in any manner except cooking, sewing, keeping a nice home and caring for my children, which I have always loved doing. In those areas he was most complimentary. "Why should I take you out for dinner when you can cook so well?" was his standard response when I would plead with him to take me out at least once or twice a year.

It would be unfair of me to say that there were no good moments in our marriage — there were many of them. Perhaps our strongest bond was a shared passion for sex. We were young and all of our glands were in good working order. But is sexual intimacy a sufficient basis for a good marriage even when in the mid-20's? Perhaps it might be for some, but a major part of any relationship must be spent out of bed. I became more and more frustrated until, finally, I was certain that I wanted out. In his own words, Don once leveled with me and uttered the cliché: "I want to keep you barefoot and pregnant."

I had two sons with Don: Don Kenneth, whom we called "Kenny," born September 17, 1942, followed by Darrel, who arrived on December 14, 1946. The life he planned for me simply was not the life I wanted for myself. There just had to be a way to make something meaningful happen with my life. Eventually, I realized that the entire solution hinged on finding a way that would be the least harmful to him and to my two sons, whom I adored. Kenny was ten and Darrell was six when the opportunity finally presented itself in the most unexpected way. To my way of thinking, any way out of my marriage just had to include a way for me to earn an independent income sufficient to support myself and my children. Little did I dream that it likewise was to include supporting an independent film-maker!

Starting in Show Biz
Chapter Two

Since I had made a successful start in the field of modeling, it was only logical that I would find a way to take advantage of the new medium of television. However, finding a way from the hills of San Dimas to the hills of Hollywood was no snap even if they were connected by the same Santa Monica mountain range. My husband actually insisted that I not venture out of the house without my mother-in-law to accompany me, even to the grocery store. Once, early in our marriage, when I accepted the invitation of a girl friend to go swimming with her at the nearby country club pool, Don actually went looking for me and found me swimming at the pool where the lifeguard had made it clear that I could swim anytime I wanted, even though I wasn't a member of the country club. Don rushed me home, took down my pants, bent me over a big wooden barrel and spanked me with a board for disobeying his "rules."

That hurt my pride even more than my butt, but of course I realized that he was jealous and wanted to keep a tight rein on me, which is what eventually drove me away. That and the fact that ten years into the marriage, I learned that he was cheating on me with one of my girl friends. Don's understanding of human nature was based on what he knew of himself, so he assumed that I would behave exactly as he did if I were given the chance. His mother was there to see that his rules were enforced when he couldn't "supervise" me himself, and one of the rules was that no man could see me or speak to me without his mother or himself being present. I was frustrated and wanted more out of life. About a hundred years earlier, Karl Marx said: "Man was born free, but everywhere he is in chains." If Marx had not been such a male chauvinist pig, he might have said the same about the plight of certain women. I just had to find a way to get out of my chains! I'd been married eleven years when the way finally opened. No other man was involved. Here is the route I took:

One day my mother-in-law agreed to accompany me on a trip to Hollywood to see a live performance of the **Queen for a Day** telecast. The program provided a woman selected from the studio audience the chance on television to have her fondest "wish" come true. At the beginning of the show, women audience members were given cards to fill out. One of the questions was "What would be your wish if you are chosen **Queen for a Day**? Some wrote that they would like to take a cruise advertised by one of the sponsors to Nassau in the Caribbean or to Hawaii; others to have a new washing machine, and so on. Emboldened by the opportunity, I wrote down, "My dream is to become a model on this show."

As a rule, I never win anything, whether door prizes, drawings or lotteries. But this was my lucky day and I came up a winner! Not only was I chosen Queen for that day, but I also won my ticket to freedom by having my wish granted. Jack Bailey, Master of Ceremonies, took my mother-in-law and me to an elegant lunch at a nearby up-scale restaurant where he told me he was choosing me for a regular modeling spot on the show — five days a week! He admired my pretty 4 1/2 size feet and decided they would be perfect for modeling the Gustinette line of fancy high-heeled marabou slippers in a rainbow of colors. Also at the luncheon was Samuel Arkoff who may have been acting as an attorney for the show or some of its personnel. I cannot now remember, but from that moment on, I was the "Gustinette Girl." My costume consisted of black mesh stockings and a short smock that showed off my long legs. With a paintbrush in my hand and a tam on my head, I held an artist's palette of rainbow-colored marabou slippers and wore a pair of the slippers on my four-and-one-half-size foot while I executed a few modeling turns. Imagine what it meant to be in Hollywood during the week with a steady income from a job that required only an hour or so of work each day! I was earning $30 per day, $150 a week, which was pretty good money for the time. In addition, this afforded me plenty of time to go on other modeling jobs, interviews, auditions, and also to explore the cultural side of the big city. I could resume the life I was beginning to explore when I was in high school and see something of that great big world that I always knew was out there just waiting for me. This prominent television spot gave me regular exposure and was recalled recently by one of my fans who bought several of my autographed photos at "Chiller Theatre" in Secaucus, New Jersey. "Chiller" is probably the largest of the memorabilia shows, attended by thousands of collectors on Halloween weekend each year. This particular fan told me that he remembered me vividly from those old TV shows and called me "the Vanna White of the fifties"! It was about at this point that my exposure and drive got me into line for my big break in the movies.

Handsome Howard Hughes had just taken over RKO and was looking for a blonde successor to Jane Russell. I had auditioned along with dozens of blonde actressses for a role in an upcoming Howard Hughes production and was personally picked by the tall, dark and intense Mr. Hughes for a part. To top off the occasion, I was invited to have a dinner meeting the next evening with him at the Nickodel Restaurant on Melrose Avenue between Paramount and RKO Studios, just to the west. My agent told me that the meeting would undoubtedly involve signing a contract for my part in the movie which I was to begin shooting the very next morning and this had us both excited. My agent, Paul Kohner, explained that it was customary for Mr. Hughes to do things at the very last minute. Paul had tried to get a signed contract when one of Mr. Hughes' assistants had first called him with the news that I had been chosen over all the other candidates, but had been told that Mr. Hughes wanted to sign me personally. We showed up early and were immediately seated in a private booth which was occupied, not by Howard, but by one of his assistants. On the table was a beautiful big bouquet of long-stemmed red roses and a note addressed to me. The note consisted of a single word, "later," and the initials "HH" which I later felt were probably scribbled by Howard's assistant. The three of us proceeded to have a lovely dinner. Then I learned that "later" really meant *much later* because a call came to the Nickodel for Hughes' assistant to the effect that Howard was tied up with business concerning problems with *Jet Pilot*, his John Wayne movie which had actually been shot by Joseph Von Sternberg about two years before. His assistant, whom

Why did I ever stand up Handsome Howard Hughes?

I believe was Noah Dietrich, was supposed to provide post-dinner entertainment by taking us to a prizefight, after which I was to be dropped off at Howard's bungalow at the Beverly Hills Hotel. Oh, oh. An alarm bell went off in my head. I must stress at this point that I really didn't know that night who Howard Hughes was. To me, he was just another producer. If my agent, Paul Kohner, had only done his job and prepared me properly, I would have known that I was in the cross hairs of America's richest billionaire, a genius and aviation hero whose fame rivaled that of Charles Lindbergh and who actually owned RKO Studios where I was scheduled to report for make-up early the next morning. How could I *not* know who he was? But I didn't and, at this point in the evening, the excitement of my dinner with Howard had greatly abated. I had absolutely no appetite for a boxing match, anyway. Not only that, but I had a seventy-minute drive to San Dimas ahead of me and I had to get up early in the morning pack my children's lunch for their school and get a good night's sleep before the ninety minute drive back to Hollywood in time for my early makeup call. The die was cast — probably in the wrong direction. I thanked Noah Dietrich and explained why I had to go home; then I headed for the parking lot followed by my agent who kept wringing his hands and telling me that I was making a terrible mistake. He pleaded with me not to leave, that I . . . "never would work in this town again" if I stood up the indomitable Howard Hughes and uttered all of the cliché arguments to make me change my mind. I told him that I would not be fit to shoot as much as a screen test in the morning if I didn't get my beauty sleep, that I had to pack my kids' lunch, and thought it much too late for a "meeting" anyway. In my own mind I was certain that I would not look good in front of the camera without a good night's rest and that Howard probably was too busy to mind if I put his movie ahead of him just this once. Wrong. I showed up at RKO the following morning and reported to makeup just a few minutes late only to be informed that the entire production had been indefinitely postponed — read "cancelled." No explanation was given. When I called Paul Kohner later that day, he rubbed salt in my wound by telling me that the part I was to begin shooting was a starring role. Why couldn't he have told me the night before? "Howard wanted to surprise you and made me promise that he would have the pleasure of seeing your blue eyes open wide." I was terribly disappointed and immediately began to think that I should have handled matters differently. What would my life had been if I had called my husband, had him get lunch ready for my children and gone with the guys to the fight and then taken Paul Kohner with me to the meeting? Surely Howard would not have minded if I had played it straight, or played along. I'll never know. After all, Howard had bought the film rights to **The Philadelphia Story** for Kate Hepburn, which turned her career around; and it is rumored that Jane Russell got $5,000 per month for the rest of her entire life. The "what if" continues to haunt me. Leaving Howard and not playing it smart became one of the great regrets of my life. Marlon Brando's line, "I could have been a contender" for **On the Waterfront** a year or two later, is apt. Brando got an "Oscar" — greatly helped by the scene where he movingly muttered that line. I had no brother to blame, only myself. Instead of a starring role in an RKO production, I got "Miss Floor Lamp of 1952." Oh, well . . .

"Miss Floor Lamp of 1952" was not the best alternative to a starring role at RKO.

For several years during this pre-Wood period, I made good money as a model, especially for shoes for some of the top name brands of shoe manufacturers, appearing at shows and on the runway and during market week. These jobs could earn me anywhere from $50 to several hundred dollars. One company, National Home Lamp Council, sent me as their model and representative to a show in Chicago where I received national attention via a widely distributed photo and promotional announcement in connection with my being named the winner of an ancillary contest sponsored by the Press and Radio Club of Chicago. This in turn led to my being sent to New York, Los Angeles and San Francisco for further modeling assignments.

Now free of financial concerns, I was free to resume my interest in motion pictures, or, more precisely, what went on "behind the scenes." This was something that had fascinated me since the age of ten when director Frank Capra was on location in my hometown of El Monte, California. My mother and stepfather Jack Glidewell were staying in the very motel where Capra was filming the "walls of Jerico" sequence for *It Happened One Night*. Capra noticed me playing with some other children and asked me if I would like to be in the movie he was shooting. Yes, yes, *yes*! I certainly did want to be in his movie. First, though, I had to ask my mother's permission. Mother came over and signed the contract, but I must admit that for the entire time of the shoot, my attention was riveted not only on superstars Clark Gable and Claudette Colbert, but on what Capra was doing. That kindly, understanding man had taken a liking to me and often had me sit near him when he was directing a scene. While there was no particular significance to my "performance" in *It Happened One Night* (I appeared only for a few seconds scurrying through one or two exterior shots as background during the motel sequence), but that Academy-Award movie did much to fixate my career objectives in the long run. Capra was a very nice man, friendly to me and good to everyone around him. He encouraged me to watch the process of moviemaking, and I was absolutely transfixed by what went into the making of a movie. I called it "movie magic" — how Capra and his crew made it rain, for instance, when there wasn't a single cloud in the sky. From that time onward, what interested me more than anything else in movies was what went on behind the cameras.

My favorite director, Frank Capra, had a major influence on film history and my own history.

My long-standing interest in dancing was wonderfully enhanced about 1951 by being given the opportunity to study with a truly great creative artist, Nico Charisse, as outstanding a dance teacher as his wife, Cyd Charisse, was as a dancer and actress. I felt extremely fortunate to get into his class and devoted myself to practicing with complete dedication. With Nico, dance was more than an art form; it was a way of life. His enthusiasm with teaching his students was contagious, inspiring and drew from me a feeling of being more alive than I had ever been before in my life. In particular, Nico taught me that my body was an instrument that plays what he called "visual rhythms" in molding physical movement to music. Now, fifty-five years after experiencing the exhilaration of his classes,

I have to struggle for the words to describe my profound feeling for the dance that so enriched my life. Toward the end of my study with Nico, one of his brothers, Pierre, began to audit the classes and selected me as his partner for exhibition bookings. We rehearsed together and built something of a reputation as a Southern California team. For a time, we were much in demand which led me to hope it might be an avenue for a movie studio contract. That did not happen but it did lead to a television contract when I was hired to work on Dinah Shore's *Chevrolet Playhouse*, one of the top-rated television shows of the 1950's. Skill in dancing was a prerequisite for the job. Dinah was the glamorous centerpiece of this popular variety show and the staging, rehearsals and professional preparation for it taught me a great deal about what goes on behind the scenes of a television show. The *Chevrolet Playhouse* required me to rehearse Wednesday and Thursday afternoons and to be on-set for the live broadcast on Friday evenings. Since I didn't have to show up until 2:00 P.M. weekdays, it made a perfect fit with my noon-time broadcasts of *Queen for a Day*.

Don Sharp was the heavyset man who hired me and gave me the responsibility to stand in as Dinah's double during rehearsals while the lighting and blocking of the show took place. Often, I played small parts on the show as well. No doubt those "bits" that were tossed my way from time to time did help me to develop as a performer, although they must have been insignificant because, looking back, I cannot remember nearly as much about them as I can for the dozens of cameo appearances that my agent got me on the Danny Thomas, Bob Hope, Johnny Carson, Red Skelton and Dennis Day shows as well as for bit parts in a number of studio movies. On *The Bob Hope Show*, where I made several guest appearances, there was the usual "Hope"-lessly male chauvinist skit. There would always be a moment where I would have to prance past in a short-skirted nurse's costume as Bob, bug-eyed, oggled my legs. Although often repeated, it always worked and the audience could see it coming — a ritualistic set-up that would be pathetically out of date today. Or would it? I have a vivid recollection of Marilyn Maxwell, well known to all insiders as Bob's steady "traveling companion," glaring daggers at me. Marilyn invariably had a major part in those shows. She had made three films with Bob and often accompanied him on his extended stints to entertain servicemen, something that endeared him to those brave boys who served our country from World War II all the way to Desert Storm. Marilyn's glare may have been part of the act, but it seemed to have genuine resentment behind it. She need not have worried. Bob seemed attracted to me (was there *any* pretty female to whom he was not?), but his reputation for misbehavior precluded any reciprocation. Sadly, Marilyn died at an early age. She will always be linked with Bob Hope in the minds of the millions who enjoyed their on-stage shenanigans.

I remember Danny Thomas with particular fondness. I appeared on his show a few times and then was up for a part in a picture he was doing and in which apparently he had some say in the casting. I was walking out of the studio one day and ran into Danny, who picked me up, twirled me around and exclaimed: "You've got the part!" Naturally, I was ecstatic, both at landing the role and Danny's genuine excitement at my getting it. But the picture business can be likened to a sandcastle built too close to the tide line. Changes were made to the script in pre-production and the next thing I knew my part was cut. Danny felt terrible and perhaps to make it up to me, he had me on his television show about six times. I saw Danny many years later, but he didn't recognize me. I suspect his memory was failing, or my many changes in hair color, hair styling and dress may have thrown him off. The extreme variation in my appearance over the years is apparent in the photos on these pages, so I don't blame Danny for not recognizing me and I will never forget his kindness to a young actress just starting out in the entertainment field.

What I recall most about Red Skelton was how he kept his guest stars and co-players on their toes. Each skit on his program was scripted, but that meant little to Red. He ad-libbed unmercifully, tossing out improvised lines that would often leave his guests tongue-tied or doubled over with laughter. I made three appearances on Red's show and he never failed to surprise me.

Ah, but the dancing! I suppose that, more than anything else but music, I have always loved to dance. Dancing has always fulfilled a deep need within me to express myself, as it has been for a great many people. Dance has been said to be the most basic physical

Danny Thomas was an admirable gentleman.

Red Skelton was completely unpredictable.

response to music that anyone can have. I know that I could never live without music. Even the most primitive societies place music and dance at the very head of their ways for expressing what is most important for their cultures. The special character of their expression defines who they are. This is also true for our more "civilized" societies. Travel the world today and you can tell a great deal about people from their dancing. Of course this is most obvious in folk dancing, but extends to theatrical forms as well. I believe that even social dancing reveals a great deal about various cultures. To the extent that our culture does the same, I believe that Gene Kelly stands among the elite few as a dancer and choreographer who have contributed to American society while, at the same time, expressing through dance what is uniquely American. It is easy to understand, then, why one of my fondest memories on the ***Chevrolet Playhouse*** was rehearsing with Gene Kelly for one of the shows. I couldn't have been more overjoyed if I had been asked to dance with the President himself. What could be better than "Dancing With The Stars"? — especially with a star like that! When I first met Gene, he had just received a Special Academy Award for his creative contributions to dance in movies and he was working on that unforgettable song-and-dance classic, ***Singing in the Rain***. Gene was at the very pinnacle of his achievement and fame, a boyish forty

Dancing with Gene Kelly was a thrilling high point in my life.

years of age. Yet he was unassuming, down to earth, professional and a complete gentleman — only slightly betrayed by a devastating smile. I saw him on a few occasions afterward at the home of my dear friend, Elena Da Vinci, and at an occasional Hollywood party, but never did he do or say anything to make me feel inclined to change the opinion I had formed while rehearsing with him on Dinah Shore's **Chevrolet Playhouse.** He was an immense credit to Hollywood and, *alas!* there have been few like him.

A Solid Start in Hollywood
Chapter Three

My work on the **Chevrolet Playhouse** paid me much more than my other steady job on **Queen for a Day** and, since I was able to work both jobs at the same time, I was soon able to support myself and my two sons. By early 1950, I had tracked down my father, Eugene Eble, who was living in Detroit. The very next day, he was on the plane to join me in San Dimas, California. Not surprisingly, he got along wonderfully with my husband and mother-in-law and his presence and emotional support helped me move forward with my plans for divorce. My father was every bit the gentleman I imagined him to be. After my grandmother had driven him away from my mother, he remarried and had two fine sons, so finding him had the additional bonus of discovering two wonderful half-brothers I had never known. They were employed in the interior design departments of the Cadillac and Ford factories in Detroit, where they eventually held key positions in those departments, retiring in the early 1990s. We still maintain close contact despite the two thousand miles that separate our households. When I bought my 1977 Lincoln Continental, Mark V, my brother Bob followed a model through the assembly line — making certain that every detail got special attention — then drove it to Las Vegas for me. I still have that car and it still handles like a dream.

Early in 1951, I moved out of my hill-top home in San Dimas and filed for divorce. Sam Arkoff offered the services of his one-man legal firm, promising to get me a hefty child support settlement, but I declined because I was making good money and did not want any sort of nasty dispute to distract me from the momentum my

My brothers, Gene and Bob Eble, held key positions at Cadillac and Ford respectively. Alas! Brother Bob died last year.

career seemed to be gathering. I agreed to take care of my sons when they were with me and Don Fuller agreed to handle their expenses when they were with him. Then I moved in with my best girl friend, Mona McKinnon, who was also going through a divorce. Mona had a lovely, spacious home in Alhambra, only a few miles east of Hollywood. I had my own bedroom, but we always shared the day's experiences and our dreams for the future in her king-sized bed. Often we would talk into the wee hours of the night and sometimes I would fall asleep there. I remember one morning how Mona teased me about waking to find me cuddled against her back, just as I used to do with my husband in happier days. She gave me a funny look and we both laughed, but I had some explaining to do.

Mona had great potential as an entertainer and, like me, had been squelched by her husband. She definitely aspired to a career in acting. She had written and acted all the parts, even those of the animals, on her own local radio show in Pomona. It was a children's program that was in many ways a forerunner of *Sesame Street* and I was certain of her talent, intelligence and future as an entertainer.

It was about this time in my life that I was introduced to the great Joe DiMaggio who, in his own way, was as much an American icon as was Gene Kelly. We were immediately attracted to one another. Joe was nearing the end of his long and incredibly successful baseball career. Without question, Joe was one of the greatest athletes who ever lived. He was native to California, but rose to fame with the New York Yankees where he set the all time record for base hits in 56 consecutive games, a record that I believe still stands. Very soon I was attending games in a sport where I'd had no previous interest.

However, my interest in the ultra-charming Joe was keen enough to overcome that handicap and the "special guest" seat that was always waiting for me helped to further stimulate my desire to learn more. After retiring and moving back to California, Joe took to sending a driver to pick me up and deliver me to the Bel Aire Hotel located in a lovely secluded canyon just west of Beverly Hills. Joe knew how to entertain and our dinner usually was served semi-privately in the romantically appointed dining room or, on warm summer evenings, on the outdoor patio.

Afterward, Joe and I would stroll through the well-manicured grounds surrounding the hotel and across a quaint little bridge, not unlike that featured in **Brigadoon**, leading to a land of enchantment.

During the games when I watched Joe play, I always admired his amazing grace in center field, much like that of a dancer. His effortless skill fielding the ball reminded me of Gene Kelly's athletic dancing, particularly in **Brigadoon** where there was less tap dancing and a lot of lyrical "outdoor" action with heather on the hills. I don't ever remember being on the dance floor with Joe, but I always thought he might make a wonderful dance partner because of his graceful moves. He was known as "Joltin' Joe DiMaggio" for his prowess with his powerful bat. Need I say more?

After our evenings together, Joe would have his driver take me home, usually with a generous token of his affection, while I sang to myself the popular song, "Joe, Joe, DiMaggio, we want you on our side!" I can't now remember exactly when it was that I found out that Joe was dating Marilyn Monroe, but when I learned that he had visited Marilyn one night after seeing me, I decided there

My romantic encounter with the great Joe DiMaggio was brief but memorable.

was no reason to continue our affair. Eventually, he and Marilyn were married and although that marriage lasted less than a year, I never saw Joe again. "It was great fun, but it was just one of those things; a trip to the moon on gossamer wings . . ." as my favorite songwriter, Cole Porter, so aptly put it.

My friend, the celebrated London artist Stephen Whately, neatly captures my career with this cartoon.

I was able to parlay my TV success into movie roles. My first part was in 1952 when I appeared with Marie Windsor in the Western, **Outlaw Women**. The next year would prove to be my busiest year in pictures. I appeared in eight movies, including **The Moonlighter**, a 3D Western that starred Fred MacMurray and Barbara Stanwyck. I received my first valuable acting lesson on the set of this picture, where I had a small role as one of the tellers in a bank that Fred and his pal, Ward Bond, were holding up. Fred took me aside and told me not to "telegraph" the slap I was supposed to deliver him because the fire in my eyes that came as a result of throwing myself wholeheartedly into the role made him duck impulsively and ruin the take. I concentrated on this lesson in preparation for the next take and Fred was able to finish the scene more or less intact. I remember being very pleased with the way the scene turned out when the film opened but not all of the distribution was in 3-D and my big scene did not make it into all of the standard 35mm release prints or the TV versions broadcast today — *alas*! I was told that one of the reasons had to do with the fact that just before my scene, Barbara Stanwyck had a scene with Fred where she too slapped his face and that scene was more central to the plot. I got my acting lesson but Barbara, wonderful actress that she was, got more exposure slapping Fred!

Some of the other 1953 movies in which I appeared included **Girls in the Night** with Shelley Winters for Universal, directed by Jack Arnold (this was Arnold's first feature, and he went on to direct many classic science fiction features during the 1950s, including **It Came from Outer Space**, **Creature from the Black Lagoon** and **The Incredible Shrinking Man**). Also, I made **The Blue Gardenia**, a Warner Brothers movie directed by the legendary Fritz Lang with Anne Baxter, Raymond Burr, Ann Southern and Richard Conte. On the set, I met George Reeves with whom I soon afterward appeared in an episode of "Superman." Also, I had a one-day shoot in Don Siegel's **Count the Hours** for RKO. I regret that we were unable to act on an invitation to attend a tribute to Siegel in July of 2005 at the Academy of Motion Picture Arts and Sciences. I also did another 3-D picture, a 45-minute short called **College Capers** (or **Campus Capers** as it was variously called) for Bob Lippert. I felt that I never looked better than in this rollicking little comedy but I

I got more exposure in Universal's "Girls in the Night."

have searched in vain for it ever since it was first released. I wanted very much to find it, or even stills, lobby cards or a poster. However, though made years after the advent of safety film, it seems to have joined the untold thousands of films made during the "nitrate era" that simply can no longer be found despite the heroic efforts of David Shepard, Roger Mayer, the Turner Classic Movies' lost film detectives, the UCLA Film Archive (which my husband,

Philip, helped establish in the late 1960's) and preservationists around the world.

In the cast of *The Blue Gardenia* there was a handsome young man with a voice like velvet. Nat King Cole was playing himself in the picture and, a few years later, I wrote a song that he would record superbly, "Someone to Tell It To." I wrote this song in memory of my dear sister, Sylvia Glidewell, who died in Havana under mysterious circumstances in August of 1957. After Mona McKinnon, she was my closest confidant.

I suppose an actor always wants to stay in "A" films, but that is not the reality of the business. One of my least distinguished efforts was as the blonde "Watcher in the Woods" in the low budget potboiler, *Lost Mesa of Women*.

Strange to say, but this weird little movie has a surprising number of devotees. Mona McKinnon joined me in that movie and our photo was featured on the cover of "Videoscope" a few years ago. She fell hard for one of the producers and they had an absolutely flaming affair which I think her husband never learned about. Certainly Mona deserved something in her life which her husband could not provide. If the affair had lasted any length of time, he would no doubt have found out about it. Mona hoped the relationship would develop in a way that would lead to a route out of her marriage but, unfortunately for her, it did not. She was not strong enough to break the chains that bound her, never left her husband and drank her way to an early death.

None of these pictures featured me in starring roles; in fact, most were uncredited bits: "Saloon hostess" in *Outlaw Women* (where I uttered my first memorable screen dialogue: "Two straight whiskeys, Barney."); "Woman at bar" in *The Blue Gardenia*; "Reporter" in *Count the Hours*. But I was still racking up screen credits, and, more importantly, enjoying the many ways I was learning my craft.

A major disappointment for me was what happened to a small but excellent part I had in a film called *The Raid*, in which I was featured with Peter Graves. That is the way I was billed by the Fox Studio publicity department. The film was based on a true event which occurred during the civil war during the 1860's. The starring roles used Van Heflin and the wonderful Anne Bancroft, with Peter and me in a somewhat parallel sub plot. I was so proud of the way

Mona McKinnon and I shared the cover of "Videoscope"

I came across when I attended the premiere with Eddie in July of 1954, but what happened when it went to television? Peter is still in the film, very briefly, but I am nowhere to be found, at least in the version that I saw when it was telecast recently. The publicity photo of Peter and me may be all that now remains of my part. What this shows about Hollywood and the movies is typical in that

They paid me well for *The Raid* and I loved being featured with Peter Graves. But how is it possible to be paid to be "featured" and then have my scenes raided in the cutting room?

it happens to nearly all actors at one time or another. I am not referring here to the sad fate of so many films before the advent of so-called "safety film" with such masterpieces as von Stroheim's **The Honeymoon** starring Fay Wray — which is probably gone forever. The pages of "The Hollywood Reporter" and "Daily Variety" are filled with announcements of film projects where principal photography never even begins. Other projects are completed and then completely disappear. I am still waiting to see **The Secret Ingredient** shot from a splendid scipt by Ric Hardman and starring the beautiful and talented Catherine Hicks. The phenomenon of "Director's Cut" reflects successful efforts to restore whole sequences that have been cut by film editors under orders of those other than the director. Thank Goodness for the DVD market, now larger than theatre box office revenues, which encourages this process.

I alternated my film work with acting in guest spots on many of the major TV shows of the day, appearing with George Reeves and Noel Neill on **Superman** ("The Wedding of Superman" episode), **San Francisco Beat** (re-titled **Lineup** for syndication), **The Damon Runyon Show** and **Dragnet**. These in addition to a steady stream of TV commercials and modeling assignments. I was a busy gal.

"The Wedding of Superman" was a wonderful TV assignment. Here I am with George Reeves and Noel Neill. The mystery of George's death has never been solved.

Breaking Loose, Enter Ed Wood
Chapter Four

One day I decided to answer a casting call in "Variety" and asked Mona to come with me. I had brought her along so that we might get her a SAG card. As I'd discovered, membership in the Screen Actors Guild was mandatory for any acting job of consequence. I had my card and had done a number of films where I was given speaking parts, though a starring role still eluded me. On that day with Mona my life turned a corner. Imagine my surprise when the interviewing producer didn't turn out to be one of those big-bellied, cigar-chomping stereotypes, but rather a man of such extraordinary good looks that it actually made me gasp. He seemed to be a cross between Tyrone Power and Errol Flynn. His name was Edward D. Wood, Jr. "Eddie" was just twenty-eight at the time, but possessed of such a winning personality and air of confidence that I intuitively trusted him. Was this a mistake? Well, it did give me pause when he told me he was "going to make me a star." During this casting call, I wore one of my best angora sweaters. I didn't notice at the time, but later I had reason to wonder if Eddie's attraction to me had anything to do with my angora sweater (hence the title of one documentary about Eddie, **Look Back In Angora**). By this stage in my career, I had been interviewed for jobs dozens of times. Most male interviewers were not in the least appealing and many were downright appalling! But unlike many of these intimidating, sexually harassing types, Eddie was a complete gentleman and played it suavely. His cool and limpid green eyes excited me and I fell for him hook, line (yes, what a line!) and sinker (oh, yes! I sure was sunk!). Almost immediately we were an item and Eddie was asking me to marry him. But I was just emerging from one marriage and, even though I soon fell in love with Eddie, I just wasn't ready to leap into another marriage. In fact, truthfully, I wasn't even ready for an affair, enticing though the prospect seemed. But when Mona and I returned home that memorable day, all we could speak about was Edward D. Wood, Jr.

At the time, Eddie was working on scripts for two or three films to star Bela Lugosi: *The Ghoul Goes West*, *The Hidden Face* and *Bride of the Monster*. Eddie assured me that I would have a starring role in *The Hidden Face* and even took out an ad in "The Hollywood Reporter" to announce it. Soon Eddie was directing . . . not a film, but a hackneyed old stage melodrama, *The Blackguard Returns*, at the Gateway Theatre on Cahuenga just north of Hollywood Boulevard. I soon learned there was nothing original about the production, including the fact that Eddie had done it several years earlier at a theatre on Sunset Boulevard.

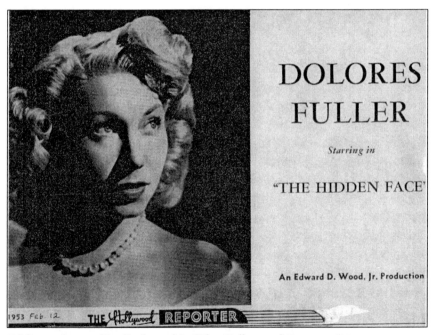

Eddie took out this display ad in "The Hollywood Reporter" to promote me and his upcoming production. The title was later changed to *Jail Bait* — a bad decision!

Eddie had Chuck La Berge interview me for a part in the non-paying, non-equity play and I went along with it because, at that point, I would have done just about anything he wanted. Our "pay" for participating in the production was pretzels (all we could eat) and beer (all we could drink, as long as we did not become inebriated and "lessen the impact of the show"). Actually, this clause of our agreement was not enforced for two reasons: those in the cast who got tipsy only added to the humor and considering how members of the audience were drinking, there were few complaints about perceived errors in dialog or delivery. Expectations were not high. It was all in good fun and everyone — cast, crew and audience — enjoyed themselves thoroughly. This little building, now called Theatre/Theatre, was utilized by Tim Burton for filming the opening sequence of his movie, although that sequence not only was off-the-wall-bad, it was a World War II drama completely unrelated to anything Eddie ever did. Perhaps Touchstone Pictures, Burton's producing entity, was unable to obtain clearance for *The Blackguard Returns* — if indeed the boys who wrote the screenplay bothered to read Rudolph Grey's wonderfully researched book on Eddie, "Nightmare of Ecstasy, The Life and Art of Edward D. Wood, Jr." (Feral House, 1992). The credits at the end of Burton's movie indicate that it was based on Rudolph Grey's book, but should have read "somewhat based on parts of the book." The tiny theatre had no dressing rooms and virtually no backstage, so we improvised by using the alley next to the theatre's rear entrance As we stood outside the Gateway Theatre waiting for our entrances, warm hugs from Eddie helped me endure the cold nights. But it stimulated my desire immensely to be so close to him and feel the warm protrusion in his trousers as he held me. The chemistry was surging through both of us and we wanted to find a place where we could be alone. But no such place was available. I would not take him to Mona's, even though she was every bit as impressed with Eddie as I was, because it simply would have been bad taste to intrude on her space. And we couldn't go to Eddie's since he was sharing living quarters with Alex Gordon, another fellow hoping to make his mark as a producer in Hollywood. We certainly were not going to go to some motel because it would have cheapened the mutual respect we were developing for each other. Also, I was extremely reluctant to "get involved" so soon out of my marriage.

But there was no stopping Eddie. He insisted on introducing me as "my wife, Dolores" to the many people we met. For instance, he told Chuck La Berge that he would appreciate it if Chuck would put "my wife" in the play. Actually, Chuck was happy to comply, judging by his remarks in Rudolph Grey's fine study of Eddie, where he was quoted as saying that Eddie: ". . . had some beautiful wives. Uh! One wife was absolutely gorgeous. I recast the show, *The Blackguard*, later on in the fifties and . . . he had a wife at the time and she was a gorgeous blonde ". . . she played the part of Lily in *The Blackguard Returns* and did a very good job."

One night after the play was over, fortified with a few free beers, Eddie talked me into coming home with him. Alex wasn't home, so it wasn't long before Eddie maneuvered me into his bedroom. I was terrified that Alex might come home, but Eddie assured me that he wasn't expected and, in any case, he would *never* come into his bedroom, a point he repeatedly stressed because there was no lock on Eddie's bedroom door. I admit that the inherent danger of the situation only heightened my excitement, already somewhere in the stratosphere. From there we just kept mounting higher and higher, finally falling asleep from sheer exhaustion.

The next morning Sam Arkoff happened to call on Eddie. Gordon has been quoted as saying that Arkoff would often come to the apartment to ". . . get himself a free breakfast." Apparently this was an arrangement made between Gordon and Arkoff to pay off legal fees Alex had incurred utilizing Arkoff's services as a lawyer. At any rate, Gordon let Eddie do all the cooking. So when Arkoff came to breakfast, Alex and Arkoff went to Eddie's door, banged on it . . . and it swung open! We woke with a terrible start and Gordon acted like the biggest prude that ever came down the pike. His holier-than-thou attitude made me feel cheap and ashamed, almost nullifying the wonderful feeling I had from the evening that Eddie and I had experienced together. It didn't seem to bother Arkoff, though.

It wasn't long after this "rude awakening" that Eddie and I got our own small apartment, just up Doheny Drive from Sunset. The apartment consisted of a small living room, kitchenette with a breakfast bar, two stools, and a bedroom. There was also a swimming pool that my sons used every day when they were with us. This was not the sort of home I was accustomed to, but we assumed it would be temporary. Most importantly, it allowed us to have some privacy. It also had the advantage of being right around the corner less than a hundred yards from my agent, Paul Kohner, whose office was on the Sunset Boulevard strip. I had selected the place in part because the proximity might help when I was up for acting jobs and needed to see Paul on short notice. At the time, Paul was the premiere agent in Hollywood, a tall, dignified man whose very presence commanded respect and whose brother Walter complemented the talent-management skills that made the Kohner Agency pre-eminent in the field.

Eddie and I were so in love that the privacy and convenience offset other considerations. We had signed the apartment lease on a month-to-month basis as man and wife and almost everything about the arrangement seemed fresh and exciting. The only thing that bothered me was when the weekends came and I wanted my youngest son Darrel to visit me. I had to pretend to my six-year old that I was still living with Mona. This involved some deception, which I hated, but my passion for Eddie at this early stage of our relationship was too great to be denied. Darrel would go to sleep on the couch in the living room of what Eddie gave him to understand was "his apartment." After he'd fallen sound asleep, Eddie and I would go to bed. I'd set the alarm for daybreak, get dressed and crawl out a small window in the bedroom; then walk along a narrow, secluded passageway that led from the rear of the building out to the sidewalk on Doheny Drive. This allowed me to come around to the front of the apartment house as if I were just arriving early from Mona's to work with Eddie. I never wanted my two sons to lose respect for me or to misunderstand and to go to their father or my ex-mother-in-law with talk about me living with some man in Hollywood.

Either it worked or it never mattered to them, for despite that deceptive/discreet behavior, my sons have always been close to me. When I lived in New York, then after I returned to California and finally moved permanently to Las Vegas — wherever I chose to make my home — my two sons have been close by. My older son, Don, now lives less than five miles away and we call upon one another for help when help is needed.

A recent event that brought great sadness to my life is the loss of dear Darrel, who suffered a fatal heart attack in September of 2004.

My sons, (ca.1988) Don (left) and Darrel, have always been close to me.

I believe that my grandson, Tommy Fuller (born May, 1992), has musical and acting talent.

Marvelous Mona was chained to a husband who never allowed her to pursue her talent.

He was only 57 and had been ill for more than a year. He had been taking Vioxx for arthritis for several years and I believe that it was a dominant factor in his demise. He left me with a wonderful grandson, Tommy, who, despite his youth (sixteen on May 20, 2008), was an immense help to his father during Darrel's final year. We are very close, for which I am truly grateful. In some respects, Tommy has replaced Darrel on my emotional horizon and I now have some of the same sorts of hopes for his future that I had for Darrel. Tommy has talent as an actor and has taken drama lessons at the John Robert Powers School. In this respect, I believe he is a "natural." He has one of the top agents in Las Vegas, Tina Hauser, who strongly endorses my assessment of Tommy. He has good speech, good articulation, good projection and an intuitive way of delivering his lines. Also, Tommy has shown aptitude for music, both with piano and with guitar. We even have written a song together. There can be no doubt about his mechanical aptitude, often demonstrated when he comes to my rescue fixing things — cars, plumbing problems, computers, the vacuum cleaners — you name it. There is no mechanical problem he won't tackle because, like his father, he loves to help.

One reason I moved in with Eddie so soon after our relationship began had to do with a situation that arose between Mona and her estranged husband, Gene. He had been living in San Francisco and for business reasons needed to relocate back to the Los Angeles area. Suddenly he needed a place to live again and made it clear that he was coming back to their home in Alhambra to effect a reconciliation. Mona begged me not to leave her alone with Gene. She was afraid that he would talk her into going back to him, which she feared would mean she would never have a life of her own. Also, she was afraid that she wouldn't be strong enough to stand on her own two feet and support herself, a much more understandable concern in the early 1950s than it is today. She was absolutely correct in her fears, but fortunately for posterity, she managed to work in three or four days of shooting in two of Eddie's films, *Jail Bait* and *Plan Nine from Outer Space*. Thus she left a modest but memorable legacy.

Gene was doing very well financially and later in life became a millionaire. But Mona wanted to pursue a career, and believed that

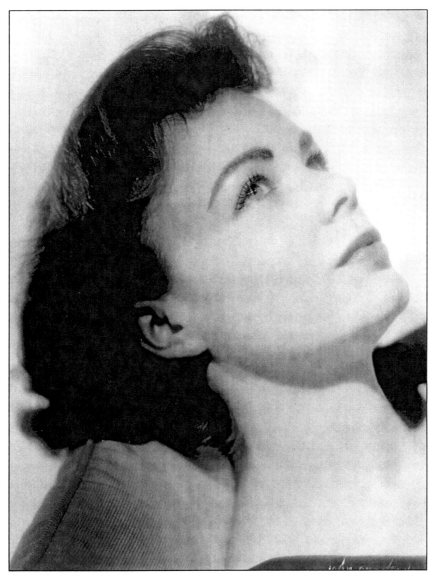

My dearest friend, Mona McKinnon, was talented and yearned to have a life of her own.

it would not be possible married to Gene. She pleaded, "Dolores, please stay with me! Don't leave me alone with Gene! He'll talk me into going back with him." But I told Mona that she would have to make up her own mind and not have me there when he came back. They did get back together and she was stuck with Gene until the day she died in 1992. She always had everything that money could buy — beautiful clothes, an upscale home, a new Jaguar. She had everything but happiness. As a result, she began to drink too much. About a year after I left for New York and it was evident that Eddie and I would never resume our relationship, Eddie cast Mona as a female lead in **Plan Nine from Outer Space**. I don't know if they ever actually had an affair, but if they did, it must have been after Eddie's ever-so-brief marriage to Norma McCarty, who played the airline hostess in **Plan Nine**. Eddie married Norma on a movie sound stage in 1956 when **Plan Nine** finished shooting. Norma soon left Eddie when she discovered him parading and masquerading in her clothes, but never filed for divorce so, technically, they were still married when Eddie was living with the woman who called herself Kathy Wood. But if living together for twenty years doesn't qualify as "marriage," it must be mighty close! There would be no question about the marriage of Kathy and Eddie if Norma had divorced Eddie because California has a common law statute, but they didn't, so the question remains. I had been told by those who knew Eddie that he had often expressed the wish to stop drinking because he could see what alcohol was doing to his good looks. I told Mona that I felt, as a friend and one who still cared about Eddie, that I might be able to help him stop drinking.

Of course Mona had been attracted to Eddie, and by the late 1950s, both sought solace from their misery in alcohol. There is a great deal of truth in the adage "Misery likes company," so the rationale clearly was there to give substance to the rumor of their relationship. Mona always shared her deepest feelings and thoughts with me, but she never intimated to me that there was anything more in her love for Eddie than a deep friendship, which, after all, is one of the highest peaks in the landscape of life. Certainly I felt that way about my friendship with Mona. We remained close till the end of her life. I often stayed with Mona in her Pacific Palisades home when I came into town from Las Vegas, where I have lived since 1968. So, naturally, I was devastated when Gene made it a point not to call me or even send me a notice of her funeral when my closest friend died. I was denied the right to attend her last rites, perhaps because Gene resented the fact that Mona and I were so close. Mona and I were best friends for nearly fifty years and I cared for her deeply. She even flew to my side in New York to

I was Linda Darnell's waitress in *This Is My Love*, originally called *Night Music*, and rented her my N. Y. apartment some years later. She died tragically in 1965.

console me when my little sister died in 1957. I wanted so much to pay my last respects to her. Last respects? No, that's the wrong term, for I will always respect her and she will always be part of me.

Knock Wood
Chapter Five

In the spring of 1953, Eddie and I had been together nearly a year. He had shot two days of an incomplete little Western nearly five years before, a twenty-minute TV pilot, along with a commercial that was never used. Nothing else.

Eddie's idol, Orson Welles, had completed **Citizen Kane** at the age of twenty-five, and here Eddie was already twenty-eight with no tangible credits. Since I had first met him, he had been working sporadically on a script called **The Hidden Face**. Soon afterward, in January of 1953, Eddie took out a half-page ad in "The Hollywood Reporter" announcing my being cast for the lead in the film. The script had been polished with rewrites and the insertion of new ideas, but no one wanted to invest money in a project by an unknown director. Eddie was itching to make movies, but we were continually frustrated in our attempts to secure financing. The community of low-budget filmmakers in Hollywood was much smaller than one might suspect, so it wasn't hard for Eddie to keep abreast of developments. Eddie was a devoted fan of low-budget independent productions, knew most of the people personally and was alert to any possibilities that might open a door for him. There had been many deals that didn't quite come off for him, but his unbounded energy and optimism never diminished.

As usual, a path to the future opens with something absolutely unpredictable. George Weiss, an independent producer Eddie knew, was bewailing his misfortune in having a "deal" fall through. The background of Weiss's deal is worth mentioning because it illustrates one sordid aspect of the picture business as opposed to, say, motion picture art. Big-budget moviemakers may look down their noses at the small independent "exploitation guys," but many of them are no different, hurrying to capitalize on sensational news events before the public loses interest or tires of the subject. "Torn from Today's Headlines" used to be a popular slogan, actually boasting of an opportunistic mentality that has characterized so much moviemaking from the very beginning. The same can be said of television, of course, culminating in the reprehensible NBC rush to get the drama of Waco out with such haste that the film set was actually burning at the same moment, April 19, 1993, that flames were engulfing Mount Carmel — church-home of the hapless, doomed Davidians.

George Weiss was able to "pre-sell" his production *I Changed My Sex* in certain rural markets because of a sensational event that made medical history, one that Weiss was quick to seize upon. That event was the first successful and widely publicized sex-change operation. It received international publicity and brought unprecedented fame to its Danish recipient, Christine Jorgensen, described by United Press as ". . . the ex-GI turned glamour girl." Weiss was Johnny-on-the-spot and got Jorgensen on the phone to agree to star in a quickie film that would tell his/her story. Weiss immediately got a graphics firm to create a one-sheet or poster for his upcoming production with a split image; the left side of the figure on the poster was male and the right side was female, representing the male/female sides of Jorgensen's persona, but without identifying any actors in the production.

But a funny thing happened on the way to Weiss's "Quality Pictures" studio. Jorgensen became a hot property, sought after by all the sleaze-ball TV talk shows of the time, and suddenly he/she wanted a better deal from Weiss. Her monetary demands kept rising with her fame. If this sounds familiar, look at any overpaid star today and see how much has changed in the last half century. Weiss tried everything he could think of to get Jorgensen to honor her telephone commitment, but to quote a famous Sam Goldwyn malapropism: "An oral agreement ain't worth the paper it's written on."

While Weiss pondered the dilemma of how to pay his/her outrageous fee and, in effect, have his pre-sale agreement held hostage, Eddie walked through the door with an offer Weiss didn't refuse. Later I learned that Eddie said something like the following to Weiss: "George, I can give you what you need. I'm the most qualified director around for this type of project because *I* change *my* sex every time I put on women's clothes." Weiss just operated on the premise that he had to come up with a film that would work with the poster he used to pre-sell his movie. Talk about a tale wagging the dog! Tim Burton's movie got this more or less right, except for the fact that Weiss was pleased with the results Eddie gave him and, unlike Eddie, made a lot of money from the movie.

Glen or Glenda? To film or not to film, that was the question.

How would you like it if suddenly the cameras were rolling on a scene in your life that reveals your innermost, secret experience? In **Glen or Glenda?**, I felt as if I were still married to my former husband, the father of my two sons, and was caught on camera in an adulterous affair. I was being tortured as much as Eddie, who was performing psychotherapy on himself, exorcising secrets that he had been hiding from me. I was torn between my love for

Eddie — wanting him to succeed — yet feeling sick as I learned the full truth about his transvestism. The time was 1953 and I didn't want any one else to find out about it. I knew he believed his big chance had come to make a picture that would be his stepping stone to success and with it the chance to make better films.

The truth is that Eddie would do anything in the world to get a picture rolling, even if it meant putting me through torture. He only showed me the parts of the script that had my own scenes. There was no rehearsal before shooting. I was merely directed to do my lines as myself and I followed Eddie's direction precisely. The style of the film was more like a documentary than a theatrical film as had been Weiss's original intention using Christine Jorgensen. I was self-conscious, angry and hurt because I did not want the world to know anything about our private lives. I pleaded with Eddie not to make me portray my own relationship with him in *Glen or Glenda?*. In turn he begged me to understand that this was his big chance. He said that *Glen or Glenda?* would never play in Hollywood, but only in Timbuktu or some backwater places where it had already been pre-sold. Eddie assured me that no one in California would ever see it and that soon it would be forgotten. Little could anyone forsee that 30 years later *Glen or Glenda?* would be a cult classic and best-selling videocassette.

We were getting paid quite adequately by George Weiss to make the film because, using the poster he had created, the film had been pre-sold to a regional distributor and there was no way he could lose so long as we brought the film in on time and on budget — which we certainly did. I finally made Eddie promise that he would use fictional names in the credits so no one would think we were telling our own stories — as if that would ever provide me with protection from the merciless glare of the media! As I recall, Eddie wrote the script in four days, which was possible because he took the central point of the film directly from our own lives. He didn't have to create an entire scenario from scratch. We shot it in five or six days to meet Weiss's deadline and the myth of Eddie's refusal to do additional takes could be traced to the very tight shooting schedule. On his next two films, I personally witnessed multiple takes whenever Eddie was uncertain that he had what he wanted. When he was happy with the take, it's true that he would call out: "**Perfect! Print!**"

Of his transvestism, Eddie had me hand him my angora and say, "Maybe together we can work it out." The photo has become a classic iconic image.

Tim Burton copied the pivotal sequence in *Glen or Glenda?* for his film, *Ed Wood,* as a tribute to Eddie. Disney used this image for a poster in Great Britain and Australia.

Eddie took the name "Daniel Davis" and I played the part of "Barbara," his fiancee from whom he was concealing a terrible secret. I had no idea of the full thrust of the script because Eddie never showed me the pages where he dressed up in the blonde wig and wore the skirt and blouse and high heels. When he did show up one day in full drag, he told me it was for a publicity photo shoot. I found it hilarious because also he was wearing his mustache. I only saw the pages where Barbara was featured. He wrote the part of Barbara specifically for me and just threw in things that related to our real life together. I was extremely reluctant to do the picture, but, in the end, my love for Eddie persuaded me to take the part because I understood that he really did need the writer-director credit. This was his first feature film effort and an altogether remarkable achievement considering the constraints of budget, time and the fact that more than fifty years later it is still being shown and making money far in excess of its original cost. I believe that there are very few films that can equal this record.

Eddie thanked me for being such a good sport to do it for him; he hugged me and told me how much he loved me and how much he needed me. He could have sold me the Brooklyn Bridge! Nevertheless, I kept wishing that we could do *The Hidden Face* first. We had that script nearly finished because we had been working on it almost since the time Alex Gordon had roomed with him nearly two years before. Eddie even took out a large half-page ad in the "Hollywood Reporter" on January 14, 1953 with my photo announcing the start of principal photography. But we were never able to raise the money to begin filming because he was without proven experience, whereas George Weiss was ready to provide the money for his project, variously known as *I Led Two Lives*, *I Changed My Sex*, *Behind Closed Doors* and, ultimately, *Glen or Glenda?*

In many ways Eddie showed his genius for improvising solutions for difficult problems with this, his very first feature. Eddie dealt with my resentment to being in the film head on. He actually utilized my feelings as material for the film itself. "Let everything show," he said. "Let it all hang out! I want everything you feel to show on the screen." And there it is today: my feelings of embarrassment, shame, humiliation, all my inhibitions and

I loved working with Eddie and here I think it shows in my face.

resentment. Eddie asked for it and I gave it to him exactly as he directed me to act for the camera. There was no rehearsal before shooting; I was just told to do the lines as myself. I complied, but I was hardly prepared. How could he write about the secrets of our life? As Sarah Jessica Parker observed, I was totally self-conscious in front of the camera. I was uncomfortable and stiff. She was correct about that, but she failed to understand, to care or to perceive *why* my performance in *Glen or Glenda?* was so stilted — yet why it was exactly right for the film. After all, this was supposed to be a reality film about two people dealing with a problem that, in 1953, was in the closet with double locks. Eddie made it clear that I was not supposed to be thinking about being an actress. "You're supposed to show how uptight you feel being engaged to a transvestite," was how Eddie explained it. Apparently, Sarah "Jurassic" Parker was incapable of creating a more sympathetic character when she portrayed my life with Eddie, and because she didn't, the result was to flaw the picture. She carried over to the Burton film an imitation of my 1953 mannerisms that were right for Eddie's film, but certainly not effective or right for Burton's film. She left audiences with the impression that I was a selfish shrew with little patience for either Eddie's movie projects or his friends when in fact quite the opposite was true. I loved Eddie, supported Eddie, shared his friendships and, most importantly, I believed in him. A large part of this problem with Parker's performance, of course, was in the script. She couldn't depart too much from the lines given her, but the emotional tone of her delivery was completely wrong because she didn't do her research and didn't understand the relationship of Eddie and Dolores.

Of the four principal roles in *Ed Wood*, Martin Landau (as Bela Lugosi) garnered a raft of awards, Johnny Depp (as Eddie) has been justifiably praised, Patricia Arquette won critical notice for her wonderfully soft, low-key portrayal of Kathy (who never actually married Eddie), and Bill Murray rendered one of his typically marvelous characterizations as "Bunny" Breckinridge. But Parker received the least satisfying press, probably because she delivered a superficial and unsatisfying interpretation of a wholly fictionalized Dolores Fuller. Parker only looked at my role in *Glen or Glenda?*, perhaps following Landau's example of copying a few selected mannerism as precisely as possible. However, what worked so well for Martin Landau could not begin to work for Sarah Jessica Parker because Bela Lugosi's highly theatrical performance in *Glen or Glenda?* was deliberate and intended to provide a commentary outside the documentary format as a frame to the central story of Daniel (Glen) and Barbara (me). But mimicking my part from that five-day production was tantamount to injecting a pseudo-documentary element into Burton's entertainment movie and thus adding an out-of-key element to the material that Burton was filming. In Eddie's original movie, Timothy Farrell played two roles: Dr. Allen (whom Inspector Warren [veteran actor, Lyle Talbot] consults in order to understand the strange compulsion to cross dress) — and the narrator. Eddie's script for this dual role is, I believe a bit too pedantic — almost boring in places. Still, the movie remains, in the words of film critic Eve Golden . . . "the only film — to this day! — to accurately differentiate between homosexuality, transvestism and transexualism; not bad . . . Wood himself was a transvestite (but neither gay nor transgendered), so this film has a kind of touching sincerity mixed in with loopy, surreal moments." Golden, I believe, got it right.

Parker chose to just portray me as a bitchy, whiny, bad actress and, consequently, the emotional range of her acting in **Ed Wood** was a little like trying to play Vivaldi's **Four Seasons** on one little piccolo. You couldn't exactly call the piccolo part "wrong," it would undoubtedly be recognizable, but one could scarcely say that a piccolo part does justice to the original orchestral score. Where Parker's acting corresponded with actual scenes in the original Ed Wood movies, a case might be made that they worked adequately. But most of her lines in the Burton movie were jarringly out of key, showing by speech and manner no love for Eddie. The film was devoid of romance, although scenes showing the relationship of Eddie and Bela showed a great deal of warmth. What then was the "Dolores" character doing in the film? Sleeping with Eddie to further her career? It would have taken very little research to verify that this was definitely not the case. Eddie and I were a team in every sense of the word. Also, I resented being shown nervously puffing on a cigarette when all my life I have passionately avoided smoking. At one time during the early 1950's, I was chosen by an advertising agency out of more than fifty girls to do a commercial for Chesterfield cigarettes at the then handsome sum of $10,000. I tried practicing a sophisticated drag but, when the time came to deliver on camera and actually inhale, I just couldn't stop coughing. No, they wouldn't accept a spoken endorsement! I only wish they had filmed me saying something complimentary, like ". . . I don't smoke. But if I did, I would smoke Chesterfields because they are the least worst!" This quote is not one I thought up, I must confess, but it fit my feeling exactly. Perhaps it's just as well that I didn't get to make the fine fee and that incident was the last time I tried puffing. There is enough air pollution today without smoking. Perhaps Parker doesn't smoke and what she did in the film was imposed on her — I have no idea. Most unprofessional and unforgivable, though, was Parker lamely trying to excuse her poor performance by saying to the media in effect: "What did you expect? After all, I was playing the worst actress in the history of film." This is to apologize for her poor critical reception by trying to shift the blame away from her flawed performance in Burton's $20 million movie to the performance of another actress (me) in a low-budget movie made more than forty years before.

In my opinion, Sarah Jessica Parker committed a "professional" cardinal sin when she never bothered to call me and talk to me, even though everyone knew where I lived. She didn't care what I had made of myself after leaving Eddie. She was playing my life yet did not do a bit of research on what kind of person I was. On the October 5, 1994 **David Letterman Show**, and when she was on four other major TV shows to "promote" **Ed Wood**, all she could say repeatedly was that I was known as the worst actress ever to appear in a Hollywood film, ever!

This personal slam was never corroborated by even the most critical reviews of my work. She just didn't get it. What she didn't realize was the torture I was going through doing **Glen or Glenda?**, exposing my secret life with Eddie. When David Letterman asked her if I was still alive and was I happy and what was I doing, she could have at least said that in my post-Ed Wood years I wrote a number of hit songs for Elvis. This information was available to her because it was right there on the screen as the end credits rolled. But she only wanted to talk about herself and ignored Letterman's question: "What happened to Dolores Fuller? What did she do with her life?" What could Parker have meant by deflecting Letterman's question with "I think I'll go home and drink a ground glass cocktail"? Had she done her research, she could have answered Letterman's questions more professionally. Clearly, though, generosity is not part of her character. On the other hand, I must give her credit

Bela did a beer commercial combined with a wrap party for one of Eddie's movies.

— or more plausibly her director, Tim Burton — for her last scene in the film, where she decides to leave Eddie. Emotionally, it was correct. Also, I have to give her credit for her subsequent business judgment as a producer of *Sex in the City*. It has been an enormous success money-wise and made her wealthy. She was astute enough

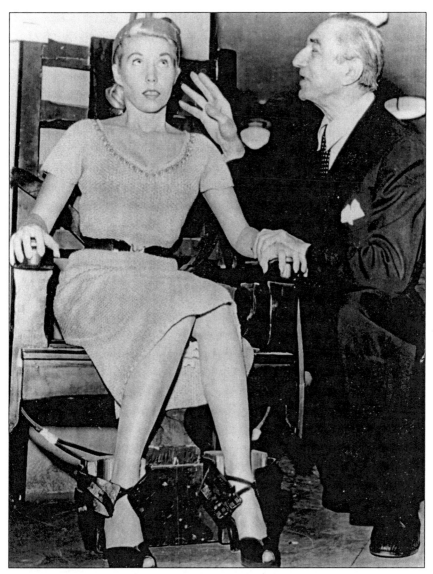

Bela and I publicized this wax museum opening, truly an electrifying experience!

to pick the lovely and talented Kim Catrall to provide the expected sex appeal in the series and for pushing the cutting edge of what would otherwise be cut out, even in the more permissive atmosphere of today's cable television market. It might be said that Sarah "Jurassic" Parker's most outstanding ability lies in her indisputable talent for self-promotion.

Sarah Jessica Parker next appeared on ***The Tonight Show with Jay Leno*** on October 11, 1994. On this occasion she made the fabricated observation that Eddie stopped giving me parts in his pictures when I could no longer contribute financially. This was a blatant falsehood. The truth is that I was making enough money from my modeling and my regular television work to buy a lovely two-story new home and a brand new Chevrolet convertible, turquoise in color with white sidewall tires and a white top. I gave Eddie my three-year old Nash Rambler for him to drive and he used it for years. It now belongs to producer Wade Williams who eventually bought up the rights to most all of Eddie's films and generated very good money, propelled by income from both the use of Eddie's films by Touchstone for Disney and from worldwide re-releases of the original movies due to interest whipped up by the Tim Burton/Johnny Depp film, ***Ed Wood.***

What I will concede to Parker is that I do not consider my work with Eddie to be very good. In fact, dissatisfaction with the quality of Eddie's work is one of the reasons that I left him, then studied with Stella Adler in New York. But to be so unprofessional as to put down another working actress who appeared in a low-budget movie made more than four decades earlier is a cheap shot indeed. How would the great Sarah Jessica Parker like to be judged on national television for her work in the first feature of a "B film director," shot in only five days with no budget for re-takes? The answer is obvious, since she has attempted to avoid judgment of her work on a long, big-budget shoot with a brilliant director who allowed her as many takes as it took to get the best he could from her. Not to mention the fact that a great deal of that footage was edited from the final cut because it just wasn't working and added nothing to the movie.

And with that, I conclude my thoughts on Sarah Jessica Parker — at least the ones I'm willing to put in this book. To go farther would be to appear as unprofessional as she, though the temptation is there because she did hurt me with her off-the-wall, mean-spirited remarks.

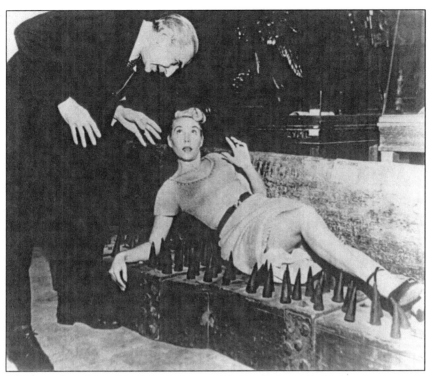

I felt comfortable with Bela, but not with Sarah Jurassic Parker.

Life with Eddie
Chapter Six

I have subtitled this chapter "Life with Eddie" because it was quite a life — a short, exciting three-and-a-half year period where our relationship grew and when Eddie's creativity was at last given a chance to blossom and be recognized . . . within existing limitations. This was also the time I was introduced to some marvelous people who became central figures in our life and in the professional career of Ed Wood.

After **Glen or Glenda?**, Eddie and I moved to a much larger and more spacious apartment that I had located in the same area of Sunset and Doheny. I carried the cost of the move and deposits, easily affordable since I was bringing in a good, steady income. As before, we signed the lease as a married couple. In the early 1950s, living together in an unmarried situation was frowned upon by "polite society" and I must confess to a certain degree of shame that I felt transgressing one of that society's most entrenched taboos. Some early writings on Eddie refer to me as Eddie's wife, but despite his repeated pleas, it was just too soon after my first marriage and I was not at all anxious to rush into another without being totally certain that it would not end like the first one. Eddie had even told his mother that we were married, sending back to her home in Poughkeepsie, New York as a memento a still from the marriage sequence of **Glen or Glenda?**, carefully altered by editing out "the Devil" character played by Hollywood agent and actor, Captain DeZita, a symbolic Best Man. The upshot was that Eddie's mother began to ask Eddie when we were going to bless her with a grand child. Certainly I loved Eddie and I was terrifically energized by the whole process of moviemaking. But entering into a marriage

Eddie cut this photo from *Glen or Glenda?* to show his mother that we were at last married.

contract was an extremely serious business and I was determined not to repeat my mistake. I did, of course (several times!), but that, as they say, is another story — several other stories in fact.

Still, I was stimulated by our sexual passion. If I am in love, as I was, deeply, with Eddie, my sexual drive hits a peak. I might still be throbbing at the thought of our lovemaking the night before but I was always ready to make love. My appetite for sex was often hard for me to control; sexy feelings were just part of me, always in my thoughts, almost as if I were in heat most of the time. I could hardly wait until the end of the day when I knew that Eddie and I would be alone together and I could satisfy my hunger. Maybe I was over-sexed, but I was young, healthy and just loved the excitement of life. And Eddie was a wonderful partner, so smooth and eager to please. Eddie had a strong, healthy body in those days, and when the mood was right for us to make love, which was often, we had no inhibitions. Eddie was an extremely talented "director" and I was delighted to take his direction in any direction it might take me. By take sixty-nine, my imagination was so stimulated I began to give direction myself! It didn't bother me that occasionally I would find my panties under his trousers because — well, I couldn't wait to pull them off anyway.

Eddie was also exceptionally accomplished on the dance floor, and one of our favorite pleasures was to visit the dance halls in Hollywood and dance to the live bands. Of course I had been dancing since I was a pre-teen, favoring ballet, and when I moved into the Hollywood area, I resumed ballet lessons with Nico Charisse, adding tap, swing, waltz and acrobatic. I believe passionately that exercise is necessary and fundamental to healthy living. This creative self-expression is mandatory for me to live a fulfilled, satisfying life. There is nothing more beautiful and sensuous than the movements of a dancer's body having sex. The arching of the back as the breasts firmly protrude and demand attention; the muscular ease of changing positions, undulating variations like the interpretation of musical tones, as strong legs stretch out embracing space, creating rhythmic patterns that bring one to ecstasy.

Eddie had studied dance under Martha Graham and he was a superb dancer. When we danced in public it was not unusual for other dancers to stop their dancing and clear the floor to watch us. It was not primarily that Eddie and I liked to show off — perhaps we did like to do that a bit, as may still be the case with many good dancers — it was more that we took a shared delight in the expressive possibilities of the dance. At home, we often turned on the record player and played music that had a strong rhythmic beat, turning our living room into our private dance studio. We'd improvise dance steps together, feeling free and filled with the desire to express ourselves. We were in love and had a lot of fun together, whether it be dancing, camping, going to the movies, or just enjoying quiet evenings at home, playing chess or working on a script. Eddie didn't drink much in those days and I always saw to it that he ate a good, healthy meal at breakfast and at night. Whether deserved or not, I have the reputation of being an excellent cook and I've maintained healthy eating habits from the time I was very young. I was considered a "health nut" long before it came into vogue for the health-minded. Another of our favorite activities was to go camping, usually in the San Bernardino mountains.

The north side of Lake Arrowhead or the area around Big Bear Lake then was especially beautiful and conducive to the

Eddie shot this color nude photo of me blending in with nature at Lake Arrowhead.

near-wilderness privacy we loved. Eddie was an excellent photographer and could handle a movie camera or still camera with equal skill. I had a Kodak "stereo realist" camera that took beautiful color transparencies in the old 3-D stereopticon format, requiring a 3-D viewer with an internal light. On a few occasions, Eddie took shots of me in the nude. I always insisted that he use my 3-D camera for nude shots so I would never fear those shots would be seen by anyone beyond my control. I discovered three of these shots only a few years ago and showed them to my sons who had never seen them before. I'm no longer afraid for them to be seen, so I have included one of them in this book. In no sense is it obscene. The color original is beautifully composed with me on a rock, almost part of the wilderness we both loved so much. Eddie was a resourceful camper and we spent many a beautiful weekend on these retreats. As the sun went down, we would pitch a little war-surplus mountain tent, big enough for only the two of us and commune with nature. Those nights under the stars, far from any traffic noise or artificial light were sheer magic, with only the sound of rustling leaves or the wind whispering through the pines. I was told by Mona that she didn't think Eddie ever took anyone else camping. If so, perhaps that sort of camping is something we shared exclusively; or so I'm inclined to think. My first husband, Don Fuller, and I used to go camping occasionally, but to camp sites with public barbecues shared by others, not to wilderness areas where we could be completely alone. Come to think of it, I don't believe I've ever done wilderness camping with anyone else but Eddie either, and the areas where we used to escape to are now relatively built up.

It tickled me how quickly Eddie could create a script from an idea, typing as fast as one would speak. His fingers would fly as his creative mind took flight. He believed in his dreams and pursued them with all of his wonderful energy. Eddie's dreams were my dreams for more than three years and I did everything I could to help him. Though possessed of an artist's sensitivity and given to moments of despondency, his basic effervescent personality made one believe that he could accomplish anything he set out to do, and he diligently tried to do everything himself when attempting to put a picture together. Of course it might have been much better if he had been able to acquire more capable help and proper financial

Bela, Eddie and me. We were a "triple threat" in the low-budget independent field. Bela's appearance in San Bernardino on New Year's Eve 1952 was wonderfully received.

backing. Although I was taking care of all the bills, allowing Eddie to concentrate solely on writing the scripts and finding financing, it was still always a struggle. Very few film directors can do it all by themselves. Orson Welles did it, certainly, but even Orson was beset by the same kind of problems that Eddie had, despite Welles' prodigious talent and the industry's most competent professional help.

I remember it was about ten o'clock one night early in 1953 after we had enjoyed a good dinner. Eddie was typing away at a speed that any typist would envy. He was working on a re-write of

The Hidden Face script. The lights were turned low and a few candles were lit, providing an atmosphere that Eddie found to be especially conducive to his creativity. We were sipping good wine and, as usual, Eddie asked for my reaction to a point in the plot. He appreciated my story sense and usually used me for a kind of literary litmus test. At the point in the script where the security guard is murdered (played by veteran actor Bud Osborne), I asked, "Honey, could you write in a part for Mona (McKinnon)? I really think she would be good on screen." I suggested that she be an employee of the theatre that is being robbed and a witness to the killing. Eddie thought that was a good idea, so he quickly wrote her into the script. As it turned out, Mona more than fulfilled our expectations and added a nice touch to the movie. Eddie even placed her prominently on the movie's lobby cards. Her screen credit also enabled her to get her Screen Actors Guild (SAG) card and do several other pictures, her best-known being Eddie's notorious, ***Plan Nine from Outer Space***. I always tried to get Mona a part in any film that I was in. Isn't that the usual custom for actors? Though not as customary, perhaps, as for men to get their favorite girls into their films — and vice versa — that a women help her girl friend in that way.

At some point one evening, Eddie asked me if he could wear my angora sweater. This was a puzzling, out-of-the-blue request, since angora was then only worn by women, and so I asked: "Eddie, why in the world would you want to do that?" Eddie explained that it would make him feel more relaxed and comfortable, that he loved the feel of angora; that he had worn angora sweaters many times before; that he would be able to write better and get into the girl's part, and that it made his creative juices flow. I was a pretty open-minded gal after all, we were living together in a common-law relationship at a time when such arrangements were generally regarded as taboo, but this revelation surprised me. I asked him how all this got started and he told me that when he was a child, his mother dressed him in a warm bunting jumpsuit that was lined with Angora rabbit fur. Angora rabbits are a special breed, raised for their long, silky hair. I loved angora myself and had at least a dozen sweaters. They were expensive, but stylish and very popular in the post-World War II era, probably because they are warm, cuddly —

and sensuous. A great many women owned at least one and often several. But men? Never!

That evening marked the moment I began to realize that Eddie had a fetish. I knew that he was all man in the lovemaking department and that he was certainly not gay or even bisexual. Actually, his reasoning made sense to me so I saw no harm in letting him wear my expensive angora sweater. If it would help him get into the mood to create a better script, well, fine. Besides, we were all alone and no one would ever find out. (Little did I dream!) At the time, I had no idea that his desire to cross-dress went any further. He loved me and didn't want to lose me so he chose to hide the true extent of his transvestitism. It was not until later that I learned his desire to cross-dress was an almost obsessive urge which was not easy for him to suppress. But suppress it he did . . . for the first year that we were together, all the while looking for the best way to let me know. Much later, it was revealed to me that on several occasions Eddie would get together with Danny Kaye to don garments from Danny's vast collection of women's costumes. They would have a ball parading and masquerading. I don't know when they met but Eddie often spoke of Danny and his brilliant wife, Sylvia Fine. When Danny was filming **Knock on Wood**, Eddie wanted desperately to visit the set and have some input because, after all, his name was Wood and he hoped to get a part in the film, or even just work as an extra. **Knock on Wood** had a lot of good routines and, certainly, was better than many of Danny's movies. I think Eddie may have watched the filming a few times, but he wasn't able to see Danny personally or even to get into a background shot.

It was during the brief, earlier five-day filming of **Glen or Glenda?** that I first met Bela Lugosi. I got to know him very well over the next two years, though I had no on-camera interaction with him. Eddie had long admired the screen classic **Dracula** and wanted him to play a role in his picture. He offered Lugosi $500 a day for his work, but Bela turned him down flat. Bela didn't want anything to do with B-movies or independent producers. After all, he'd been in quite a few films with Universal, one of the top studios. Additionally, the film's subject matter did not particularly appeal to him. But Bela soon relented. He needed money and in those days no one wanted to cast him, so he agreed to do the picture *if* his salary were doubled. Bela's popularity had peaked in the mid-30s, after appearing in such classic chillers as ***Mark of the Vampire*** and the triumvirate of movies in which he co-starred with his "rival" Boris Karloff: ***The Black Cat***, ***The Raven*** and ***The Invisible Ray***. Sadly, following the British ban on horror movies, his career began a downward spiral from which it would never recover. By the early 1950s, no one was offering him work — except Edward D. Wood, Jr.

Bela's personal life had also taken a bad turn when his wife of 20 years, Lillian, divorced him, taking Lugosi's only son, Bela, Jr., with her. Bela married five times in his life, but Lillian was the one wife he truly loved and their divorce devastated him. I adored Bela, and I believe the feeling was mutual. Our more spacious living quarters above Doheny enabled me to invite Bela to have dinner with us, which he did often during the next year and a half. Bela always appreciated our invitation to a home-cooked meal. He particularly loved my Hungarian goulash that I prepared from a superb recipe given to me by my Hungarian grandmother. The recipe is incorporated in one of the songs in my stage musical with Scott Martin. Scott deserves primary credit for this song and he created the synthesis of recipe for the goulash with a recipe for friendship which neatly encapsulates what developed with Bela, Eddie and me during the many times we three got together for dinner, conversation and planning our future projects. Once shooting began for the three films that I did with Eddie, we often were joined for dinner by cast members. On these occasions, it was more customary for me to serve my spaghetti special with marinated meatballs that had a sauce requiring a full day's simmering. Bela loved this dish almost as much as my goulash which was especially appreciated also by Theodora Thurman and Lyle Talbot, as I recall. During pre-production of ***Jail Bait***, Eddie arranged for Bela to make a personal appearance on New Year's Eve at a theatre in San Bernardino, at that time requiring a drive of about an hour and a half east of Hollywood on Interstate 10. The three of us drove there in my new Chevrolet and when Bela strode on stage attired in his Dracula cape and tuxedo with tails, the crowd went wild. The theatre manager and his wife were delighted, promising to run ***The Hidden Face*** when it was released and inviting Bela to return for an opening night promo. At that time, Eddie planned to use Bela for the role of my father, Dr. Boris Gregor, but of course this never happened because Bela was held over repeatedly in the booking Eddie got him at the Silver Slipper in Las Vegas. Universal Pictures may not have wanted Bela in 1954, but the public demand for Bela had not abated. Bela and I made several promotional appearances during this period when we were close friends. One that I remember vividly was for the opening of the Hollywood Historama, forerunner of the Hollywood Wax Museum. Two photos of us were widely distributed: one was with Bela hovering menacingly over me on a bed of spikes. The spikes were made of rubber, true, but they were definitely uncomfortable. The other photo taken by Nate Cutler of "The Globe" shows Bela trying to make me comfortable in the Museum's electric chair, an artifact used in *Angels With Dirty Faces*, as I recall. The photo was also run by Forest J. Ackerman in an early issue of "Famous Monsters" with the caption: "Electrifying chairman, indeed, is Bela Lugosi, whose celebrated movie villainies usually get three jeers from audiences. Here he has pretty Dolores Fuller in his clutches. They're co-starring in *The Ghoul Goes West*." Eddie thought the cross promotion for his movie would help find money to get from the pre-production phase to actual filming. Indeed, it may have helped Eddie to get into serious discussion with Gene Autry, whom he had high hopes of landing for the leading role. I was told later that Alex Gordon, who had introduced Gene to Eddie in late 1951 when they were living together, spiked the deal because he had become jealous of Eddie's success in making *Glen or Glenda?*. Alex remained close to Autry for most of the rest of his life and had an important position in Autry's fabulous Western Museum, located near the eastern edge of Griffith Park in Los Angeles. Eddie was generous toward Alex, nevertheless, and gave him co-writing credit for the script of *The Hidden Face* and for *Bride of the Monster*, even though Alex's contribution was minimal, merely telling Eddie about an idea for *The Hidden Face* that he got from a low budget production, a 1935 gangster picture called *Let 'Em Have It*. Alex did none of the actual writing on the script and I'm likewise not certain that he made any significant contribution to *Bride of the Monster*.

Although Martin Landau gave a standout performance as Bela Lugosi in Tim Burton's film and he certainly deserved his Academy

The Hidden Face, released as Jail Bait, was Steve Reeves' first film role.

Award for Best Performance in a Supporting Role for his work, his highly creative and unique portrayal of Bela as a broken, embittered, caustic old man was not the way I remembered Bela — quite the opposite. Bela was always the perfect cultured gentleman whom I never once heard use obscenities. In my opinion, the real Bela, while not as "contemporary" as the excellent fictional character in Burton's *Ed Wood*, was deeper, more compelling, more complicated and, I think, far more interesting, although perhaps not as amusing. I grew to love him and to respect him enormously as a human being. He was such a sweet, gentle soul, kind and considerate in the

Veteran actor Herbert Rawlinson took the part originally intended for Bela Lugosi as my father.

extreme. To this day I have wonderful memories of Bela with my seven-year old son Darrel on his knee, telling him stories in that deep, magical, enchantingly accented voice. Later he, Eddie and I would stay up until quite late discussing moviemaking and our plans to make other pictures together. Those were the days that ***Bride of the Monster*** was on the agenda, in which I was to star with Bela but which was not to be. The casting intrigue would eventually contribute to my breakup with Eddie.

Another keen interest that Eddie had was chess, at which he excelled. Somehow, during the move to the house I bought at 1039 North Valley Street in Burbank, Eddie's chess set was misplaced. He wanted to teach my son, Darrel to play, so he took him down to the five and dime store which didn't have chess sets. There he bought lots of little toy soldiers and other miniatures, then proceeded to make a set from scratch. It was a creative solution that worked well and that little home-made set got lots of use.

There are those who scoff at the idea that Eddie was in any sense a creative artist, but during my years with him, I was surprised almost daily by his creativity. One example that comes to mind is the series of five 1954 Christmas cards he created. I had been a 3-D enthusiast for many years and had my own "Stereo Realist" camera, made by Kodak but discontinued in the early 1960's. It was a time when 3-D was enjoying one of its periodic fads, so we decided to go all out and make a series of tableau-like 3-D cards. The shoot was done at my two-bedroom Burbank home where Eddie and I lived with my father. The series of 3-D shots for the cards utilized our entire "family" and ranged thematically from a naughty shot of me in an abbreviated Santa costume for a card inscribed, ". . . the night before Christmas," through a card with my father as "Santa Claus" toting a big toy-stuffed sack and son Darrel reaching excitedly for one of them, to a nativity scene in the stable with friends as the three wise men, Eddie as Joseph and myself as the Holy Mother, to a stunning shot of Eddie as a mature, bearded Jesus, arms outstretched in supplication and the inscription, ". . . lo, I am with you always . . . " It is an eerie coincidence, writing this in June of 2007 and without realizing it a few years ago when I wrote the song for **Ed Wood . . . But I Wouldn't** telling Eddie in the form of a letter why I was compelled to leave him that the song was entitled "Always With You"! Could it be that deep within my subconscious mind I had retained the memory of Eddie's inscription taken from the New Testament on that Christmas Card created more than fifty years before? In any case, I know the words to be profoundly true and the sentiment profoundly felt.

I guess it is to be expected that I would defend **Glen or Glenda?** even though I almost never mentioned it in my credits because I identified more with my work in "A pictures" and aspired to have more work in major studio productions than in "one lung" independent productions. Fifty years ago, independent productions were almost synonymous with "B" pictures. In those days, there were only seven major studios which formed an elite circle with very little contact with the independents. The independents usually had little contact with personnel working in the majors and maintained their own circle inhabited by such as Alex Gordon, Ed Wood, Samuel Arkoff, Steve Apostolof, Ron Ormond, George Weiss, Ronnie Ashcroft, Fred Olen Ray, Roy Reid, Anthony Cardoza, David Friedman and Joe Robertson. These people and "B" picture actors, script-writers and other personnel usually were ignored by those who wrote about movies until recently because public interest leaned far more in the direction of the major studios and the elite circle of directors, actors and other, more prominent, film folk. I think this state of affairs promoted a caste mentality that affected the way the "B" picture people were seen. No doubt it affected me as well because I desperately wished to make "A" pictures, especially musicals. I didn't mention my Ed Wood movies because I tended to look down on them. All of this changed with the release of **Ed Wood**, starring the amazing Johnny Depp and the eminent Martin Landau. Furthermore, the director was no less than the hot "A list" Tim Burton who was just coming off his box office triumph, **Batman**. Releasing the film was Buena Vista, Disney's distributing arm. I was thrust into the limelight and had to change my viewpoint. If film authorities such as Professor Albert Johnson are enthusiastic about "B" movies, who am I to disagree with them? Even film reviewers and academics were embracing the "B" movies. A reviewer for the "Village Voice" in New York was quite extravagant in his praise for **Glen or Glenda?** when Paramount released it in the spring of 1981 following the urging of my old classmate, Warren Beatty: "Eons ahead of its time, the film is a passionate defense of transvestism — and thus free expression." This quotation comes from an excessively erudite article by Chris Cooling entitled "Ed Wood, Glen or Glenda and the Limits of Foucauldian Discourse." The article begins, "although he is currently a cherished and beloved cult icon, Edward D. Wood, Jr. remains a distressingly under-appreciated director," and then proceeds to "examine" the movie in the most over-intellectualized manner imaginable. Frankly, I didn't know what he was talking about most of the time and I doubt that Eddie would either. The Medved brothers were having fun when they tried to put Eddie down. They helped Eddie instead. But woe to Eddie when pretentious academics start taking **Glen or Glenda?** so seriously. Foucauldian discourse indeed! That is nothing less than the death of the spirit.

During two guest appearances I had on the 1954–1960 TV show **San Francisco Beat** (also called **The Lineup**), I played the wife of a handsome man, Dudley Manlove, who was a chess champion. Since I was in San Francisco for about ten days owing to other work between guest appearances, Dudley took me to dinner on

Fisherman's Wharf several times. Dudley was an excellent dancer and had taught ballroom dancing, so it was inevitable that we went dancing nearly every night and enjoyed a brief, delightful romance. After all, I told myself, I'm not married to Eddie and Dudley is attractive, cultivated, interesting and seductively attentive. Of course I told him about Eddie and what an excellent chess player he was. Shortly after that, Dudley came to Los Angeles. He was a staff announcer for NBC Radio in San Francisco where he was very well known. Dudley was the voice of Lux Soap commercials and acted

Dudley Manlove was handsome, attentive and had a wonderful, radio announcer's voice.

Eddie was handsome, attentive and had a fixation on my angora sweaters.

in *Dragnet* episodes as well as episodes of *Alfred Hitchcock Presents*. Since I had no intention of continuing the relationship with Dudley, I introduced him to Eddie and almost immediately they became fast friends. Eddie admired his wonderful, low-pitched baritone voice and asked Dudley to narrate a radio monologue that he wrote called "The Final Curtain." Also, of course, Eddie used Dudley in *Plan Nine from Outer Space* where he played "Eros," the right-hand man of the Supreme Ruler, played by Bunny

Breckinridge, with great gusto. We played chess a great deal with Dudley, usually alternating with him because Dudley almost always won whether playing against me or against Eddie. Like Eddie, Dudley was fond of drinking and one morning, after playing and drinking all night, Eddie and I went to bed, and Dudley, in no shape to drive home, crawled into our big double bed on the opposite side from Eddie. There I was in the middle with Eddie completely passed out and Dudley snuggled next to me with something on his mind other than sleeping. It was not easy for me to ward off his affection because at that period in his life, I found him extremely attractive. But ward it off I did. Dudley's interest in me continued, but the timing was never right and I left for New York in the fall of 1955 where I was swept up in a new, exciting life. Dudley faded in and out of my life and the timing never again was right — if it ever was.

It is no secret that Bela had a drug problem, but it must be remembered that his addiction stemmed from a medical necessity. He wasn't "shooting up" for kicks. Bela's addiction was very much the same as that of Howard Hughes whose use of morphine began with the terrible plane crash in Beverly Hills. Howard refused to allow the resulting pain to stop him from working so he resorted to ever-increasing reliance on morphine. I remember only once watching Bela "take his medicine," as he euphemistically put it. He was at our apartment and in a great deal of pain when he took a little pan and started boiling water to sterilize a needle. He gave himself the injection and the whole procedure was done very quickly. I'd never seen anything like it and I had to ask Bela how he'd got started on this. He said that he suffered severe leg pains from an old World War I wound and that when appearing in a stage production in England he was in such pain that he couldn't go on stage until a doctor was summoned who gave him an injection of morphine. This was repeated from time to time until it reached a point whenever Bela would begin to feel unbearable pain, he'd give himself a shot and feel better. Well, on that night in our home it certainly did the trick, because soon Bela was up and around, smiling and congenial as ever, giving no hint of the suffering he'd been enduring only a few minutes before. Eventually morphine became a problem for Bela and, in a courageous move, he committed himself to a hospital for treatment, where he underwent a complete cure just one year before he died. Howard Hughes never lacked courage but I suspect that he lacked Bela's self-awareness and discipline to do anything about his dependency on morphine.

Bela was just one of our many friends from this period. Eddie attracted people because he was fun to be with and very creative. In particular, Eddie's enthusiasm was contagious. I have fond memories of big Tor Johnson who, despite his enormous size and intimidating presence, was a kind, soft-spoken man — though with a Swedish accent so thick it was often difficult to understand him. The casting of George "The Animal" Steele as Tor Johnson in Burton's *Ed Wood* was right on the mark. If Vickie Thomas was responsible for this inspired bit of casting, she certainly deserves a ton of credit. Likewise for Bill Murray as Bunny Breckinridge. His hilarious, subtle underplaying was perfect and caught the essence of flamboyant Bunny who came into Eddie's circle later, but whom Eddie enjoyed and worked into his movies. The real Bunny was different in many respects, but Bill Murray had very little to go on and created an unforgettable character, a unique individual of uncertain gender. Vincent D'Onofrio was utterly perfect as Orson Welles, although to my knowledge Eddie never actually met Orson. This was apparently another scene created for dramatic effect in the Burton picture. Lisa Marie sought out Maila Nurmi, took her shopping and studied her work with excellent results for her subsequent screen role as Vampira. Certainly, Lisa Marie had the right physical qualifications for our friend, Maila, even though Maila never truly became part of the Wood camp. Incidentally, Maila is the niece of the world-champion Olympic long distance runner, Pavo Nurmi, from Finland and was a girl friend of Orson Welles who, alas, gave her the clap! This is revealed by Maila in the documentary, *The Haunted World of Edward D. Wood, Jr.* (still available on VHS or DVD). The talented and beautiful Patricia Arquette, received very favorable mention playing "Kathy O'Hara," partly because she took Kathy to lunch and got to know the person she was playing, so her acting carried conviction. As long as we are on the subject of who played the parts of our circle in the Tim Burton production, I must make further comment on Sarah "Jurassic" Parker who never took the trouble to call me and got the character of "Dolores Fuller" entirely wrong. It is rumored that Johnny Depp was annoyed with the way she was playing me, vowing never to work with her again. It is evident from her acting that her inherent mean-spiritedness could not be covered up in the movie. I was told by a telephone operator at one of the hotels where she stayed on a shoot here, that she was arrogant, demanding and just plain nasty to the hotel help. Obviously, she has the best face that money can buy, although I get the feeling when I see it that it might melt and drop off if she is ever caught in the rain. She has made a fortune selling sex — granted that it is the beautiful, sexy and talented Kim Cattrall that attracted the male audience to her HBO show. Credit someone's business acumen to the fact that Parker gets all of the money from re-runs and residuals of **Sex In The City**, but it's no credit to Parker because there is no generosity of spirit in evidence. The deal ruthlessly deprives Kim and the other two actresses from receiving future income from six years of their work. The same selfishness was displayed by Parker on national television when she trashed me unnecessarily and even refused to answer David Letterman's question about what I had done with my life. She gave me no credit for anything and struggled for a way to keep attention on herself, clearly a driving ambition she has found ingenious ways to fulfill for many years. The September, 2005 issue of **Vogue** has Parker on the cover. How did that happen? **Vogue** of all things! But many other covers, too — way out of proportion to her importance as an actress or television personality. Now she even has her own perfume. What a smell! Those who admire her should try it.

Paul Marco, who perhaps became most famous for playing "Kelton the Cop" in Eddie's movies, was our devoted friend. Paul took his screen name from Kelton Avenue where he once lived in Hollywood.

Paul threw a Christmas party for Bela in 1955, complete with a black Christmas tree! Paul should have been given a token role in Burton's flick, but there was a misunderstanding that precluded his participation. In 2005, a short film was made showing Paul in his world. It is called **Kelton's Dark Corner.** While it was not nominated by the Academy's short films branch for an "Oscar," there are those who feel it should have been.

RIGHT: **Bela, Paul Marco and me at Paul's party for Bela at Christmas, 1955.**

BELOW: **Conrad Brooks and me at "Chiller Theatre" in 1997 with my last angora sweater.**

There were others in Eddie's circle of friends, such as former B-western bad man Kenne Duncan whom Eddie used in several films. Another long-standing friend was Conrad Brooks, first used by Eddie in a little home-movie that was never released and later cast in *Glen or Glenda?* in a minor role. Actually, all of the Ed Wood movies with Conrad used him in minimal roles, even when he joined with Paul Marco in *Plan Nine* as another cop. Conrad got his best shot, in my opinion, in a major role as the ominous butler paired with the weirdly memorable Johny Link in *Ironbound Vampire*, written, produced, photographed and directed by Karl Petry. Another member of our "family" was the self-styled psychic, Criswell — also well cast and memorably portrayed by the versatile Jeffrey Jones. "I predict" he will long be remembered.

Harry Thomas was an outstanding make-up artist who befriended Eddie and me about the time we were working on *Jail Bait* and who continued to work with Eddie on several other movies that Eddie made. Harry was a delightful, sensitive man who loved to sing and who even wrote a few songs that I felt might have been popular if recorded by a well-known singer and promoted properly, which is the key to the success of any song. It was true in the 1950's and is still true today. A few years ago, Harry wrote me a letter about Eddie's decline which shows the closeness they had: "We were working on *Revenge of the Dead* which I had a great time doing with a lot of fun make-up stuff. Eddie came by one day after shooting and we had a drink or two. Eddie never drank during work but he sure made up for it afterward. That day he was depressed, which was unusual for Eddie. He kept saying, 'Harry, what happened to my life? I used to have everything — my beautiful wife, Dolores — we did everything together — she even helped me with these shoots — what happened to my life? Where did I go wrong?' The poor guy even broke down and cried and there wasn't anything I could say to help." Harry is gone now, too, but the memory I have of that sweet man that sticks in my mind is from a time about ten years ago when the interest in Eddie was at its height and several of us who worked with Eddie were gathered in a hotel room, I think it was in Palm Springs during their film festival. Harry was softly singing one of his songs for us and smiling all the while. It was a touching, beautiful moment and everyone there was quiet, listening intently and appreciating how Harry was enjoying the attention.

Another friend and a true professional coup for Eddie, was his director of photography, William C. Thompson, who was responsible for the beautiful look on most of Eddie's early films. A Director of Photography, or DP, as the term usually is abbreviated, is the highly experienced professional who supervises the work of cameramen and gaffers on a production. Not only was Bill Thompson a D.P., he was a member of the cinematographers branch of the Academy of Motion Picture Arts and Sciences. This exclusive branch is the smallest of the fourteen branches of the Academy and, even today, includes only about two hundred members. To my knowledge, Bill never won an "Oscar" but he was justifiably proud of his Academy membership. There was a period when *Glen or Glenda?* was unfairly judged by inferior VHS tapes illegally copied from television broadcasts which themselves were made from second-rate, second or third generation sources. I firmly believe that Eddie's choice of professionals for his movies proves that he would have done very outstanding work if he has been able to attract sufficient financing. He almost did this with his casting of Gene Autry opposite the evil Dr. Acula (in what was to be a Republic Pictures production of *The Ghoul Goes West*, but when Autry dropped out, so did Republic. Hollywood is littered with the corpses of stillborn and aborted productions. To my way of thinking, this type of abortion is far worse than the kind now being opposed by right wing political thinking. Perhaps half of the publicity releases announcing film projects that are sent to the trade papers are never printed and another half that are printed never get out of pre-production. Many that are finished never open in theatres. They are still "in the can" or go straight to video. Now that high resolution DVD earns as much for a movie as box office returns, many movies are planned exclusively for DVD release from the beginning. Everything changes except the old rule that "movies follow the market." Or, as Harry Cohen said, "Give people what they want." Was that why so many industry people showed up for his funeral? Or was it, as Sam Goldwyn said of an unpopular colleague, they came to the funeral to make certain that he really was dead?

About 1980 or '81, when my old Stella Adler classmate, Warren Beatty, was at Paramount making his great Oscar-winning film about John Reed, *Reds*, that he wrote, produced and directed, he talked Paramount into acquiring *Glen or Glenda?* Warren had the idea that Paramount should release the film on the midnight circuit where he felt it would become a long-term smash in the vein of *The Rocky Horror Picture Show*. I'm not sure the idea was a good one because Eddie's film was very different. While it had its own share of transvestism, it was not a spoof of the horror genre but a serious plea for tolerance; not a kinky theatrical comedy but an almost documentary exposition of its subject. It probably would not have succeeded at that time in the 1980's even if it had the specialized kind of promotion that Paramount simply was not equipped to deliver. Paramount approached the project correctly by buying the best pre-print material from George Weiss and striking several 35mm trial prints for release. While the advertising campaign was adequate, the promotion was not and the experiment bombed. The left-over 35mm prints were acquired by Wade Williams about 1994 and released in an astute campaign that followed first run showings of Burton's *Ed Wood*. It was here that *Glen or Glenda?*, *Plan Nine* and *Bride of the Monster* performed their best and did extraordinary business worldwide. Anyone who saw the screenings of these 35mm prints must have been astonished at how good the screen images looked, considering the word-of-mouth reports from those who saw inferior tape copies and earlier telecasts.

By 1954, my movie career appeared to be advancing. My agent, Paul Kohner, landed me small parts in four pictures that year: *The Playgirl* with Shelley Winters, *This Is My Love* with Linda Darnell and a somewhat more substantial role with Van Heflin, Anne Bancroft, Lee Marvin, Richard Boone and Peter Graves in the Civil War drama *The Raid*. Unfortunately for me, my sub-plot romance with Peter Graves was too close to the one that was featured with Van Heflin and Anne Bancroft and therefore was eliminated during the final cut. This was also the year when Eddie finally made *The Hidden Face*, released with an ill-advised exploitation title, *Jail Bait*, which backfired to the film's box office detriment. There was a line in the script in which my screen character, Marilyn Gregor, told my brother that he should not take the gun with him because it was "jail bait." The distributor seized on this term for a release title because he thought it might bring more people into theatres. However, in 1954 the term was understood to mean an under-age girl with whom someone was having an unlawful sexual relationship, therefore risking a jail term. The film's new title was misleading for those who went expecting a salaciously slanted story, therefore creating negative word-of-mouth. In actuality, *Jail Bait* was a good example of '50's *film noir* with an ingenious plot twist. Also, it was the first film to star Steve Reeves and that made me his first leading lady. I received second billing under veteran actor Lyle Talbot, although on posters and in some of the advertising, even recent video and DVD covers, my name comes first. The DVD copies are quite good, but many film reviewers avoided writing about this movie because it didn't allow them to ridicule Eddie. Even Leonard Maltin's "Movie Guide" staff refers to *Jail Bait* as "less inept" than Eddie's classics, a back-handed compliment if ever there was one. Once *Glen or Glenda?* was released and made money, getting funds for *Jail Bait* was much easier. J. Francis White and Joy Hauck had a chain of theatres in the south and to insure a supply of "product," they formed a producing company called Howco Productions which put up the money and gave Eddie sufficient time to do the film properly, although Ron Ormand, their supervising producer-director, pressed Eddie to begin filming as soon as the finances were in place. Ron had been the producer of a low-budget "B movie" in which Mona and I had small parts. During the filming, the handsome and charming Ron began an affair with Mona which lasted through the filming of *Jail Bait*. Eddie and I often had dinner with Ron and Mona, usually in one of the better Hollywood hotels with a dance band where we enjoyed our favorite pastime. Mona fell hard for Ron and confided to me that she hoped it would lead to a way out of her stultifying marriage. but Ron's busy schedule with Howco kept him away from the Los Angeles area for long periods of time, so he and Mona drifted apart. The publicity for this film led to the best notices I ever received for any of my film roles and one of them was both flattering and typical of the exaggerated hype that streams endlessly out of Hollywood to persuade people to buy movie tickets: ". . . Beautiful, blonde, Dolores Fuller who stars in

Ed Wood's Testimonial Benefit screening of *Bride of the Monster* for Bela Lugosi was held May 11, 1955 at the Paramount Theatre in Hollywood. Shown here are Allen Nixon, Maila Nurmi ("Vampira"), Tor Johnson, Lincoln Theodore Perry ("Stepin Fetchit"), Bela Lugosi Jr., Paul Marco ("Kelton the Cop") and myself. Eddie took the photo; the press was absent.

Jail Bait, celebrates on screen her third picture for Howco Productions. After commendable roles in ***Mesa of Lost Women*** and ***Outlaw Women***, the voluptuous, shapely, talented Dolores was asked if she would like to play a really different type of role. Dolores accepted and it is now predicted from this staring vehicle that Dolores will go a long way in the motion picture world." Reading this more than fifty years later, I feel inclined to gag myself with a spoon, as the saying goes. "Commendable" roles? "Insignificant" roles would be more accurate!

Jail Bait was fun and an inventive shoot, in which I played no small part. Besides starring as the female lead, I also performed what might be termed appropriately as associate producer duties. My modeling work provided additional benefits much appreciated by Eddie. Westwood Knitting Mills (for whom I was their sweater girl), suit designer Gene D. Evans and a lingerie manufacturer, Chick and Pandora, agreed to supply the wardrobe for the women on all the films that Eddie made while we were together. This was in exchange for screen credit. *Jail Bait* was probably the Ed Wood film that utilized the most gratis female clothing. I just picked out the outfits that were needed for all of the women in our cast, and they even let me keep the clothes once we were finished shooting — I suppose mostly owing to my promise that they receive screen credit. Another of my duties on *Jail Bait* was helping Eddie secure the various locations used in the film. We charmed the Sheriff's Sub Station at Temple City, the Alhambra Police Department and the Hollywood Branch of the Los Angeles Police Department into letting us film exteriors of the police stations for some shots and the booking desk for some interior scenes. They even furnished cop cars and some uniformed officers for atmosphere. The fire department also cooperated by letting us use some fire trucks in a scene. Also we were given permission to use the Monterey Theatre in Monterey Park for the robbery scene in the picture, where my friend Mona played the girl who witnessed the crime. These "freebies" helped keep the cost of the movie low and enable Eddie to bring the movie in on time and under budget.

Our greatest location challenge was finding a suitable nightclub. We spent a lot of time going to many places before we found the Hunter's Inn nightclub in Temple City, with a twenty-foot ceiling that was needed for the camera crew. Then we had to convince the owner that we were going to make the Hunter's Inn famous because of all the publicity he would get by having a movie shot at his nightclub. Fortunately, as it turned out, it really did create more business for the owner, owing to very good local promotion. During the filming, my father, Eugene Eble, was living with Eddie and me in the home that I had bought on North Valley in Burbank. He was very helpful in many ways, allowing us to concentrate on the shoot. My father got along famously with Eddie so it was no surprise when Eddie asked him to play the part of the bar tender at the Hunter's Inn. Although he had no previous acting experience or training, we thought he did a fine job and I've taken a great deal of pleasure in seeing my father in this brief little part years after his death.

One of the reasons the production excited me was because Bela Lugosi was slated to play my father, Dr. Boris Gregor, a noted plastic surgeon who turns the tables on the gangster who murdered his son. Unfortunately, Bela couldn't get out of a contract that Eddie and my agent at the time, Lou Sherrill, had landed him. Eddie, Bela and I flew to Las Vegas for the opening at the Silver Slipper in Las Vegas where he was headlining "The Bela Lugosi Revue." We rented a car after arrival to avoid taxi fares. At rehearsal, I met comedian, Hank Henry, who was working up a routine with Bela and who was known at the time as "Mr. Las Vegas." Hank and I became friends and through those years we did some promotions for a little airline known as "Air Pony Express" that flew people to Las Vegas. I was hired to do publicity wearing a scanty cowgirl outfit. I remember once when I arrived from Los Angeles the weather was so cold that I had to wear my full-length mink coat over my meager costume and stand on the wing of the plane with Hank while the photographers shot pictures of us. It seems that most of my life, I have avoided exposure to cold air if at all possible. I even wrote a song for the airline which was used to promote it on local radio wherever Air Pony Express originated flights to Las Vegas — chiefly Orange County, Los Angeles, San Francisco and San Jose, California. At one point, that little song was running on about ten radio stations but, needless to say, it never made the "Hit Parade." Hank worked very well with Bela, respected him as a thorough professional and they got along fabulously — contrary to the impression one may get from the Tim Burton film. Bela was trained as a Shakespearean actor and had vast experience on the stage where he first made Dracula a hit, leading to his definitive screen role. Later, we visited the "Bela Lugosi Review" after it became a Las Vegas success. We drove the long and in those days arduous journey over terrible roads. Now, of course, there is a beautiful interstate freeway for Las Vegas to tap the money of southern California which, perhaps, is why some have called Las Vegas an exurb of Los Angeles (an exurb may be defined as a place beyond the suburbs).

Bela's contract had an excellent clause which allowed the show's run to be extended if the producer so wished. Little did Eddie imagine that the show would be such a success that it kept on being extended, thus cutting our dear friend, Bela, out of the shoot for **The Hidden Face** when Eddie's funding came though. And so, Bela was replaced by veteran actor Herbert Rawlinson, an MGM star who headlined many top studio productions as the lead during the late silent era of the 1920's. This casting of top Hollywood talent demonstrated Eddie's generosity toward those who were no longer in demand and whom Eddie believed should not be passed by simply because they had gone out of fashion. As the Hollywood saying goes, "you're only as good as your last picture" . . . the epitaph of many fine film folk. The brilliant Frank Capra, for example, who had more impact on the development of movies in the 1930's than probably any other director, was unable to get a movie made after his box office failure in 1960 with *Pocketful of Miracles*, starring Bette Davis. And so it was consistent with Eddie's respect for veteran actors that he turned to Herbert Rawlinson when Bela was tied up in Las Vegas. Sadly, when Rawlinson completed his scenes, he died almost immediately of lung cancer, which made *Jail Bait* his swan song.

Steve Reeves made his film debut in *Jail Bait* as Lt. Bob Lawrence. Steve, though incredibly handsome and already possessed of the physique that within a few years would win him international fame as *Hercules*, was somewhat awkward before the camera. He was always more comfortable without a shirt. I remember it took him twenty-seven takes to tie his tie. Yes, when Eddie was not rushed to finish filming, he would not hesitate to re-shoot a scene. Between takes, Steve would sit with me, sharing talk about the importance of exercise while munching on dried fruit and nuts — appropriate because we were both called "health nuts." Steve and I would occasionally meet a few years ago when we would both be at celebrity signing sessions staged by Ray and Sharon Courts at Beverly Garland's Holiday Inn Hotel in North Hollywood. Still exercising two hours every day, Steve was the picture of good health when I last saw him in 1999, so it came as a complete shock to learn that he died in the spring of 2000 of lymphoma. Steve and I had a kissing scene to do in *Jail Bait* which I was really looking forward to, but when we filmed them, there was just no chemistry. Possibly the lack of chemistry came because Steve, in his first film, knew that Eddie and I were "an item" and felt it best to play it safe — a gentleman first and a police lieutenant last. In any event, the editors, Charles Clement and Igo Kantor, took this sequence out of the completed film. Charles Clement was another example of Eddie using top talent. Charles worked in the sound department at Universal Studios and later was elected to the Sound Editors branch of the Academy of Motion Picture Arts and Sciences. Charles came to the U.S. from Belgium and, among other memorable French language films, he created the English sub-titles for the Marcel Pagnol classic, *Regain*, starring the great French comedian and character actor, Fernandel. The subtitling of foreign language films is an art apart for it goes far beyond translation of dialogue, especially when dialogue is fast. Straight translation would never allow enough time for audiences to read all that is said in a rapid exchange of ideas. Much creative thought is required to convey the essence of what is said in a few brief words and Charles Clement was one of the best with that special talent. Igo Kantor went on to produce quite a few successful low budget movies, as did another Ed Wood alumnus, my friend, Ted V. Mikels, who directed me in two of his productions during the 1990's. One of Ted's films, *The Doll Squad*, was the predecessor of the television series "Charlie's Angels," but not even so much as a thin dime came to Ted. Not that it was an exact copy of Ted's concept, but it was close enough to cause everyone who saw Ted's film to realize where it came from.

Lyle Talbot, who played Inspector Johns in *Jail Bait*, worked in well over a hundred movies throughout his career. During the early 1930s, he had been a big star at Warner Brothers, appearing in such films as *20,000 Years in Sing Sing* (with Spencer Tracy) and *Three on a Match* (co-starring Humphrey Bogart and a young Bette Davis). You could always depend on him to turn in a good performance. As with Bela and Herbert Rawlinson, Lyle's career had slipped during the 40s and 50s, so he was delighted when Eddie offered him a part in *Jail Bait*. For his part, Eddie was fortunate to have a consummate actor like Lyle in this and other films, including *Glen or Glenda?* where he played another policeman, Inspector Warren. Eddie and Lyle became good friends, and occasional drinking buddies. One night the doorbell rang at 2:00 A.M. It was Lyle and it was obvious that he'd had a lot to drink — so much, in fact, that his wife, Lillian, had locked him out. Lyle had been quite the "man about town" in his younger days and Lillian wasn't sure where he'd been. Lyle asked if he could sleep on our couch, which wasn't the first time for that scenario. He had a lovely wife and young son, but Lillian wouldn't put up with Lyle's drinking. I recall once when things had gotten quite out of hand, Eddie and I appearing at a hearing for their impending divorce. During the hearing, their eyes met and you could see they were still in love. Lyle reached out for her hand and promised then and there not to drink any more. Lillian wanted to give him another chance. Their reconciliation must have worked because they had four children and stayed married until Lyle died at the age of ninety-two in 1996. His last on-screen appearance was with me in Brett Thompson's feature documentary, *The Haunted World of Edward D. Wood, Jr.* (1995).

To my mind there is little question that *Jail Bait* is the best of Eddie's films. It is a more polished production that exhibits thoroughly professional performances from its players. The story line is taut, suspenseful and surprising. It is just so unfortunate that Eddie was never really able to duplicate this success (though he did come close with *Bride of the Monster*). Eddie wrote the script for *Bride of the Monster* while I was with him and especially crafted the role of Janet Lawton for me so that I could work with my dear friend, Bela Lugosi — which I had been longing to do. Plus the role of Janet Lawton offered me far more opportunity to act than anything I had done before and, if I had been able to do that picture with Bela, I believe it would have helped my acting career. I was studying, becoming more self-confident, certain that I could now display my talents as an actress. Not that *Bride of the Monster* would have enabled me to realize my ambitions for stage or screen. The high tide of MGM musicals was already receding after 1954's *Seven Brides For Seven Brothers* and it was beginning to be apparent to me that Eddie's interests were not in that direction, nor in the sort of "A" pictures that would have given me scope — ones that would have enabled me to "live" the part and project the sorts of emotion with dramatic intensity that I believed I was capable of. Alas! Eddie simply was never going to even try to make a main-line Hollywood movie. To make matters worse, we were having difficulty funding *Bride* despite several promising luncheon meetings with prospective backers at the Brown Derby. As a rule, I got to pick up the check. There was one backer named Lou Snyder who kept trying to put his hands on my legs under the table. No doubt he was trying to see how much I'd be willing to compromise in order to raise money for the movie. But it didn't take a genius in human psychology to see that Lou wasn't the type of money-man one would want our company to get into bed with. Me neither!

Then we heard that a young lady interested in films had inherited some money. We set up a meeting with her at the Tail o' the Cock restaurant on Ventura Boulevard in the San Fernando Valley, just over the hill from Beverly Hills. When we arrived, Loretta King was sitting at the bar, but not drinking. We offered to buy her a drink but she refused, saying that she didn't drink liquids because she was afraid it would put weight on her. Being more of a health nut than a diplomat, I informed her that she should drink eight glasses of water a day to keep from drying up like a prune. This, needless to say, did not exactly get us off to a roaring start. This important meeting was distorted in the script Tim Burton chose to film, showing Eddie meeting alone with Loretta. It had never happened that way, but including my character in that movie-meeting just did not serve the dramatic purposes of the script-writers, Scott Alexander and Larry Karaszewski, whose first treatment done with minimal research had been embraced by Tim Burton. After all, the project was never conceived as a documentary, so my criticism that the movie departed from the real story is of course purely personal and outside objective evaluation of the motion picture as an entertainment for the general public. I truly believe that the real story would have been better, deeper and more interesting than the fictional lives portrayed, which is one reason why my stage musical **Ed Wood . . . But I Wouldn't** has attracted such interest. But that, as they say, is another story.

Back to that meeting at The Tail of the Cock: Loretta asked Eddie how much the picture was going to cost and Eddie said that we could do it for about sixty thousand dollars. I distinctly recall Loretta saying: "Really! That doesn't sound like very much." This much is faithfully included in Burton's shooting script. Eddie and I took this remark to mean that she could easily handle financing the project. Big mistake! She looked over the script and immediately focused on the starring part of Janet Lawton that Eddie had written for me. My heart almost stopped right there.

When Eddie informed me later, after other meetings with Loretta's agent, Marge Usher, that she would be doing the part of Janet Lawton, I was hurt and angry. What had happened was that Marge Usher wanted me to sign with her agency. But I had been with the Kohner Agency since the beginning of my career and felt a strong loyalty to Paul and Walter Kohner. Marge responded to my refusal by manipulating her client Loretta King into the role intended for me by finding production funds from her own sources. Thus, I learned another lesson for those interested in what goes on behind the camera: The Golden Rule — Whoever has the gold makes the rules.

Angry? I was furious! Not only had Eddie promised me the part, but it had been announced in the trade papers that I would be co-starring with Bela Lugosi in *Bride of the Monster*! It was late at night. I jumped into my car, gunned the engine and "peeled rubber" as I left Eddie in a cloud of dust. I headed up the hill to Mullholland Drive that winds across the top of the Santa Monica mountains. I had driven in a few drag races just for the thrill of it when I was married to my first husband, Don Fuller, who raced as a hobby. He had taught me how to take a curve at top speed: brake only occasionally just before the curve, then accelerate around turns and brake when necessary on straight stretches of roadway just before the turns. I was in a semi-suicidal mood of not caring what happened to me so I flew across that serpentine mountain road at full throttle in a frenzy of frustration. But somehow I eventually came down to earth after a few close calls with calamity; I calmed myself as best I could and drove back home.

I was so disappointed in Eddie for not fighting for me by insisting that he would be doing the movie *his* way. He tried to console me by telling me that he would write me a better part, but there was an ache in the pit of my stomach that was more than physical. Losing the chance to co-star with Bela really hurt, but I was determined to see the picture through to the end and not leave Eddie high and dry with something that meant so much to him. When it came time for Loretta and me to do our brief scene together, Eddie didn't try to block our mutual hostility, but used it to drive the exchange. Loretta made it clear from the delivery of her lines that she was no friend, on screen or off. My character "Margie" handed it right back to her.

The bit part had been thrown to me as a bone, but I made the best of it. Viewing that scene some fifty years later, it does show a certain crackle. The sarcasm in my voice was actually flaunted, so, once again, Eddie displayed his talent for seizing opportunities around him to benefit his movie, although I did not appreciate it at the time. This scene was another that was precisely copied by Tim Burton as a tribute to Eddie. What I especially did not appreciate was Loretta's reneging on her implied promise to help finance the movie. At one point, the man who owned the studio where the picture was being filmed appeared on the set demanding to be paid. So Eddie went over to Loretta and asked for the rest of the money to complete the movie (she had given him a rather small amount to get the picture rolling). But that was it. More recently, I learned that Loretta actually had inherited some money but under conditions of a trust that prevented her from squandering it. So, when Eddie asked Loretta for the rest of the money, she replied with some surprise:

"What money?"

"The money we contracted for," Eddie said.

Then she dropped the bombshell. "I don't have any money."

At the time, I was livid and believed that she had tricked Eddie into giving her the part he had written for me and now he was left high and dry without the cash to complete the picture. Worse still, Eddie allowed it to happen without taking into consideration all the loyalty I'd shown him. From financially supporting Eddie, to taking care of his physical well-being, to assisting him in every way I could to see that his movies got made, I thought of myself as a full partner, only to discover that this was really not the case. I began to question the future of our relationship and slowly came to the conclusion that I had to move on to better things and not continue to think that I could advance very far if I stayed with Eddie. Perhaps I felt that he had stopped growing and I had not, even though I was nineteen months older than he. Those three years and several months with Eddie were wonderful in many ways but, as with Don Fuller, it was just that I wanted more from life. Especially, I wanted a partner who would always treat me as an equal. He might be more than an equal in many ways. I would like to look up to my partner, but please, never make me feel looked down on or treated as less than one deserving of full confidence.

Years later, I learned that Loretta King's agent, Marge Usher, found the man who supplied the completion funds. His name was Donald McCoy. McCoy owned a meat-packing company and had no experience whatsoever in making movies. But putting up the much-needed money entitled him to become Executive Producer, and one of his first orders in this capacity was to get his inexperienced son Tony put on the film as Associate Producer and also cast in the romantic lead role of Lt. Dick Craig. Yes, Eddie really compromised to get **Bride of the Monster** made, but, as they say: "Whatever it takes . . ." I attended most of the shooting at Griffith Park (which provides the climax for the film and where Lugosi's mutated Dr. Vornoff battles an octopus before both perish in a Donald McCoy-dictated "atomic explosion") and appeared on the set while my hurt festered. Tony McCoy was having an affair with one of the girls associated with the production — I think it was the script girl. They could hardly wait until the end of the day's shoot to go off to a nearby tool shed and get it on — probably practicing a little meat packing. They would come out covered in dirt, straw and cobwebs, smelling to high heaven. The whole thing disgusted me and at one point I asked how they could stand such conditions, how could they even consider it without cleaning up first? Of course there was no place in Griffith Park for the girl to douche and they even boasted that the raunchy odors only added to their sexual turn-on. Ugh! So much for the meat-packer's son.

After the film was completed in late March of 1955, there was a cast party in Donald McCoy's meat-packing plant. This was the only occasion that I saw Eddie appear publicly in women's clothes. At the very end of the party, Eddie disappeared for a few minutes, then returned, making a sensational entrance by coming out dancing in full drag. He wore a long blonde wig and sexy women's clothes, padded brassiere and wrap-around silk skirt that showed his legs. Incongruously, this feminine image was contrasted with his usual moustache. He entertained everyone. Everybody was laughing — except me. I was embarrassed. Maybe I hadn't had enough to drink to appreciate how "hilarious" it was. Cute as Eddie was, it did offend me and we had a rather heated exchange about it later. This scene was well staged by Tim Burton and accurately depicted the event and how I felt about it. I knew that night that it was over between Eddie and me. In addition to his "betrayal" in giving Loretta King my part in the picture and flaunting his transvestitism that night, Eddie had also started to drink heavily, and I've never had much tolerance for anyone who abuses alcohol. Perhaps his drinking stemmed from his disappointment in himself for allowing his control of the project to be manipulated away from him. Still, I stuck it out until after the benefit premiere for Bela on May 11, 1955. Reluctantly, I had the locks changed on my house in Burbank. Then one evening around sundown Eddie showed up quite drunk and stood outside the house crying, "Dolores, I love you! I love you! Please let me in! I love you!" It was a very sad scene. I'm sure the whole neighborhood heard him. I knew he really did love me, and this left him broken up. But the time had come for me to move forward, and it wasn't long afterwards that an opportunity presented itself that would set my career and my life in a whole new direction.

Before the **Bride of the Monster** premiere, Eddie had to come up with the lab fees. He couldn't do this so he went to the meat packer, Donald McCoy, who had already spent more on the film than he intended when Marge Usher originally approached him. He then told Sam Arkoff about his predicament. Sam had seen the work print and had been pleasantly surprised with what Eddie had accomplished. So Sam came up with the money, but there was a terrible price: Eddie had to give Arkoff ownership of his film in exchange for money the lab required to hand it over. Eddie had little choice. He wanted to help Bela by putting on the benefit premiere, so he reluctantly made a deal with Arkoff. It was a bad deal all the way around because the premiere was not properly promoted and failed to take in the sort of money Bela needed. It was the following year before **Bride** could be distributed to theatres and Bela's final performance was seen, but general release then was through Arkoff's new American International Pictures. With good promotion, the film was successful at the box office so it would not be off the mark to say that AIP was launched by the Ed Wood productions, although Eddie was never cut in on the profits. There is another way that Arkoff benefited from his association with Eddie. Arkoff took careful note of the successful promotion of ***Glen or Glenda?*** George Weiss began with an idea, dreamed up an exploitation title, then had a poster created to illustrate the title. Finally, using the poster as a sales tool, he pre-sold the film in certain territories. Once he was assured of distribution, he got Eddie to write a script and direct the movie. When Arkoff's American International Pictures started producing some of the pictures they were distributing, ". . . Arkoff and cohorts would think up the title first and then come up with a poster to sell the title. Only then would they order a writer to come up with a script to fit the title and poster" (from an interview and article on Arkoff in the publication, ***Insight***, January 26, 1987). Arkoff had great success with this formula, to which he added his great skill in finding the most effective way to market his films to his "B-movie" target audience. They were cheap exploitation movies taking two weeks to shoot. Arkoff had nothing but disdain for the art of film; for him it was strictly a business of providing a product for an immature audience of mostly teen-agers, as is abundantly clear from his most notable success, ***I Was A Teen-Age Werewolf***.

As of this writing in mid-2006, I am completing work on a stage musical with my partner, Scott Martin, a brilliant musician who on occasion comes up with fine, imaginative contributions to my lyrics. At the finest of the celebrity signing shows and specialized film festivals, "Monster Bash" in Pennsylvania, which is held annually, I was a guest of honor on June 24-26, 2005 and played two modest demos from my forthcoming musical which tells the true story of my life with Eddie. Appropriately, it is called ***Ed Wood . . . But I Wouldn't***. The Monster Bash audience gave the playing of both songs an enthusiastic and rousing round of applause. One of the songs comes near the conclusion of the musical as a letter that I write to Eddie telling him why I had to leave him. It encapsulates the way I felt leaving Eddie and is entitled "Always With You." My lovely friend, Barbara Bogar, sang the demo, accompanied on the piano with great professional panache by Scott Martin. Her photo and my lyrics follow.

LEFT: **Barbara Bogar, booked internationally by the Jay Ramsey Agency in Las Vegas, sings exquisitely.**

I spread out my wings from my need to fly higher
From the need in my heart to move on,
I feel so young that my dreams are on fire
My decision feels right, right or wrong.

I flew 'cause I knew of a world that is waiting
Anticipating my songs, always with you songs
Hurtin' and blue songs
And I know I have to be strong.

I have to find out just how far I can go
On my own. I have so much to learn
The friends that I know will help me to grow
And I can't promise you I'll return.

There's a tug at my heart and I find a tear falling
I can still hear you calling my name.
There's a love in my heart that I'll always remember,
And a place that is always with you.

I left Eddie, but he never left me
Chapter Seven

Paul Marco was a co-player in Ed Wood's films **Bride of the Monster**, **Plan Nine from Outer Space** and later the semi-sequel to **Bride**, **Night of the Ghouls**. In all three films he essayed the comic character of "Kelton the Cop," the role for which he is best known by his fans. Paul has been a favorite at film collector conventions, where he frequently appeared to sell his autographed photos, as he has also done on his Internet web site. Shortly before his death in May of 2006, Paul recalled to Stone Wallace those early days working with Ed Wood and me:

> "She was a beautiful girl and I remember that she always supported Ed and treated him with great kindness. She was modest and always nice to people — the cast and the crew. There was never display of temperament. I felt she never really received her due as an actress. But I'm very proud of the success she achieved through her other endeavors."

Not playing the role promised to me in **Bride of the Monster** remains one of my great professional regrets, particularly since it would have afforded me the opportunity to share scenes with Bela Lugosi in his last substantial film. After Bela's treatment for drug addiction, he appeared in a small role as a mute in director Reginald LeBorg's **The Black Sleep** and made his final screen appearance posthumously in silent footage Eddie spliced into **Plan Nine from Outer Space**. These pictures hardly do Bela justice. I personally feel that it was his role as Dr. Vornoff that served as a fitting finale to a memorable career. Perhaps Tim Burton felt the same way because he put a great deal of emphasis on Bela as Dr. Eric Vornoff in his movie, **Ed Wood**. Burton even staged a wonderful repeat of the speech Eddie wrote for Bela that Martin Landau faithfully copied and powerfully delivered near the end of the film. I believe this heart-rendering speech and the way Burton staged it was an important factor in winning Landau his Academy Award as "Best Performance by an Actor in a Supporting Role." This Oscar was awarded in the spring of 1995 for the 1994 year. *Alas!* that Bela himself was never awarded an Oscar, not even for his landmark performance as Dracula. Another role for which he was so deserving of a nomination was Ygor in **Son of Frankenstein**, where he so brilliantly cast off the cloak of the vampire and truly became the evil, cackling broken-necked shepherd. But his is not alone among the memorable performances that failed to win the prized golden statue. The Academy rules allow for five nominations for male supporting performances, five for supporting female performances and five each for "best" actor and actress performances. With five nominations, it does not take much thinking to realize that nearly six thousand votes by qualified members can easily split support between two superb but less popular performers thus enabling a popular but less artistic performance to receive more votes than either of his two competitors. On balance, the most praiseworthy performance may usually prevail, but Oscar prediction is not an exact science. Las Vegas odds-makers are never 100% accurate. My husband, Academy voting member, Philip Chamberlin, insists ". . . there is no such thing as a 'Best Performance,' only a consensus of preferences among Members who vote on any given year. Never mind the wild card that makes it seem unlikely all Members who vote on any given year see *all five* of the nominated performances, although the Academy and producers of nominated films take pains to provide Members with every possible encouragement and opportunity to see them. Given how tastes vary among voting members of the Academy and members of the voting public alike, it seems inevitable that disagreement will always exist where 'winners' are concerned. It's enough that five of the finest are nominated by their peers." At the annual "Monster Bash" on June 25, 2005, a well-known Lugosi impersonator, Michael Thomas, re-enacted a scene from **Bride of the Monster** with a huge, six-foot, eight-inch impersonator of Tor Johnson who brought the scene to an end by presenting me with a lovely bouquet of flowers. All five hundred members of the audience recognized the scene and responded with thunderous applause. Eddie would have loved this tribute to his work.

Although Eddie continued to make movies, the quality of his later productions rapidly deteriorated until they resembled the most amateurish of home movies. I don't think it was because I wasn't there to help him. I was told that his drinking made him appear unreliable in Hollywood. Also, his passion to make movies never abated and he would take any opportunity to shoot a film. By the late-1960's he was reduced to writing and/or directing low-budget porno films. In one of these, **_Take It Out in Trade_**, he even played the role of a transvestite, Alecia, in a humiliating sequence. To pay the rent and buy booze, Eddie wrote from thirty to seventy screenplays for others to direct and literally hundreds of short stories for such salaciously sensational publications as "Pendulum," "Calga" and "Gallery Press" magazines.

After we parted in 1955, I never saw Eddie again. I understand from interviews in Rudolph Grey's exhaustedly researched book "Nightmare of Ecstasy" that he stumbled into an alcoholic and moral fog and died homeless and in poverty. At one point when I had returned to California in 1964 and was speaking with my dear friend Mona McKinnon, I told her that I wanted to find Eddie to see if there was anything I could do to help him. Mona's reaction was strange; she didn't want me to see him, and was quite adamant about it. Perhaps I should have been more insistent, but I respected Mona's wishes and left it at that.

All of Eddie's personal torment and professional discouragements finally ended on the morning of December 10, 1978. He was barely fifty-four when he suffered a fatal heart attack. It was such a tragic end and so inconsistent with the wonderful memories I have of Eddie in his prime. That's why what happened next is so ironic and bittersweet.

In the early 1980s, a forgotten Edward D. Wood, Jr. was "rediscovered" through the efforts of Harry and Michael Medved. Harry, the younger of the brothers, had written a book that became a runaway success called "The Fifty Worst Films of All Time."

Rudolph Grey and me at "Chiller."

While Eddie's work did not receive a scathing sarcastic review in this first publication, he rose to "prominence" in the follow-up volume, "The Golden Turkey Awards." Not only did Eddie win the dubious distinction of being named "The Worst Director of All Time," but also his film ***Plan Nine from Outer Space*** was labeled "The Worst Movie of All Time." Of course this verdict was not the result of any ballot or consensus but of a clever notion that such a gimmick would help sell the book. Perhaps it did. But the Medveds' label came across as an attempt to make fun of Eddie's work. Instead, the designation had the reverse effect, primarily because of interest stirred up by such an outrageous designation, parlaying off the already substantial following built around the late night television showings of Eddie's films. First, an admittedly poorly conceived "bad movie" compilation, ***It Came from Hollywood***, was released, with a special segment hosted by comedian John Candy saluting the work of Ed Wood. Then Michael Gavey came from England to do

The Son of the Incredibly Strange Film Show. This hour-long documentary began appearing on the Discovery Channel, followed soon after by Rudolph Grey's definitive book on Eddie, "Nightmare of Ecstasy, The Life and Art of Edward D. Wood, Jr." (Feral House, 1992). This book went into several editions and was translated into German, Japanese, French, Italian and Russian. Film rights to Grey's book were purchased by Tim Burton's company because first, the book was a bestseller for Feral House; second, Burton had been a longtime admirer of Ed Wood; and third, he liked the treatment brought to him by Scott Alexander and Larry Karaszewski.

I understand that the script was written quickly, within about six weeks. I wish they had taken a little longer and done better research. But six weeks was a long time for a script by Ed Wood standards! While Burton's movie was not a commercial success, everyone now knew of Wood the man and maverick movie director. Rhino Home Video rapidly sold out its wonderfully conceived and edited Ted Newsom documentary *Look Back in Angora*, which hit video shelves in 1994, close to the release of the Burton film. Tower Video had a similar success with its release of *Jail Bait* and from time to time there have been thousands of back orders for *Glen or Glenda?* waiting to be filled in video stores, the demand exceeding the supply. Superbly remastered DVD editions of *Glen or Glenda?* and *Bride of the Monster* have been issued with excellent accompanying commentary by Rudolph Grey. Meanwhile, *Glen or Glenda?*, the movie Eddie had promised me would never be seen by a wide audience, has played all over the globe with *Jail Bait*, *Bride of the Monster* and *Plan Nine from Outer Space*, often collectively out-grossing the Burton flick! These three actually were combined in an angora-clad box! Also, the impressive feature-length documentary film *The Haunted World of Edward D. Wood, Jr.*, directed by Brett Thompson, appeared on the festival circuit in 1995. The August 7, 1995 issue of "Variety" carried a highly favorable review after its enthusiastic reception at the Munich International Film Festival. Most notably, the film set an extraordinary box office record for documentaries during its one-week limited theatrical run at Goldwyn's Nuart Theatre in Los Angeles in May of 1996. This led to more theatrical bookings than any other documentary had enjoyed in years.

Director Brett Thompson and I on the set during the filming of his definitive documentary, *The Haunted World of Edward D. Wood, Jr.*

Frankly, I was astonished and bewildered by this phenomenon. How many directors can you name who have been the subject of a movie? We cannot count ***What Price Hollywood?***, that wonderful 1932 George Cukor masterpiece — and the first of four versions later called ***A Star Is Born*** — because Lowell Sherman's role was that of a *fictional* film director. No. Except for some documentaries, I can't offhand think of another movie. Like the title character, ***Ed Wood*** may be unique. Certainly there is a lot to admire about Eddie. Tim Burton has been quoted as saying that he ". . . can also relate to Wood's spirit. He had such a passion for his filmmaking that it didn't matter to him what other people thought." There is a universal aspect both in the film and in the film-maker. Eddie's love of the motion picture medium and his constant struggle to overcome lack of funding to get his projects made is something that many of today's hungry young filmmakers can relate to. So often, when I've spoken with those who have seen Eddie's movies, the conversation comes around to Eddie's ingenuity in finding ways to get something made inexpensively. After all, isn't it the concept that counts most of all? Realization certainly is important, but it isn't everything. So many movies today are brilliantly executed. We marvel at the technique and are spellbound by the way production problems are solved. But all too often, it is the triumph of form over content.

I was drawn to Eddie almost as much by the chance to get behind the scenes of the magical moviemaking process as I was by his extraordinary good looks and innate human sweetness. Also, there is at least one fascinating contradiction within Eddie himself. He was "all man," as I've had occasion to say before. On the other hand, how can one explain his odd compulsion to wear women's clothes? Does Eddie somehow represent the full range of human sexuality? Why does the enigmatic figure of Ed Wood continue to have such strong appeal to both men and women? Perhaps there are no answers to these questions and yet there are many more questions that could be asked! But one thing is certain: more than a quarter century after his passing, Eddie haunts us by achieving a sort of immortality. If not identical to our own immortal aspirations, at least in one unexpected and unforeseeable heavenward spear-thrust, he has overcome death. Isn't this the ultimate purpose of life? The only things that really matter in life are those that outlive us. Some have gained immortality by writing poems, some by painting, some by building edifices of beauty, some by raising children who survive us and join an unbroken human chain down through the generations . . . and some by making movies.

Storming New York

Chapter Eight

"Going back to the old Ed Wood stuff that Dolores had done; there was a short circuit there. If it hadn't happened, I feel she would have gone much further in the acting area."

— MARTIN LEEDS,
FORMER EXECUTIVE VICE PRESIDENT OF DESILU PRODUCTIONS

I left the perpetual sunshine — if stiflingly creative environment — of California for New York in the fall of 1955, when I was offered a job modeling shoes for a big company. In a way, I was going back to my beginnings, but I really didn't feel I was taking that much of a step backwards. Despite a flurry of bit parts, I hadn't advanced as much as I would have preferred in my acting career, even with my leading roles in **Glen or Glenda?** and **Jail Bait**. Of course **Bride of the Monster** remained a bitter memory (it still is). Besides, the modeling pay in New York was $50 a day — not bad money back then. I was met at the airport by a friend, director Stanley Kramer, who personally drove me into Manhattan. This was my first trip to New York and I must admit that to say I was impressed would be an understatement — the George Washington Bridge, Radio City, Times Square — the city seemed alive with opportunity and I instantly felt that I could do well here. It was the right place to begin the next phase of my career.

My first big opportunity in New York occurred when, after a few weeks, I had briefly returned to Los Angeles. Broadway producer Julie Stein was in California auditioning for someone to replace Jayne Mansfield as the lead in the Broadway play, **Will Success Spoil Rock Hunter?** Jayne was committed to honor a movie contract that conflicted with her Broadway scheduling in **Rock Hunter**. "Hollywood" has always been bi-coastal and is now global. I know that Julie saw dozens of girls, but he selected me to fill the bill. The show called for a sexy gal with a drop dead figure which Julie

Stein recognized in Jayne and me so I immediately flew back to New York to begin rehearsals. This was an exciting opportunity — my potential "big break" after years of doing Eddie's pictures and small parts in mainstream movies — and I worked hard to perfect the role. I had not seen Jayne's performance in rehearsal and, since it was a brand new show that not yet been presented, I felt free to create my own characterization without any preconceived idea of how Jayne might have been interpreting the role. I was immensely excited during the weeks of preparation and rehearsal. However, to my disappointment, Jayne managed to get out of her movie contract and fulfill her obligation to the show, which became a smash hit. She performed on-stage every night and I never did get the chance to fill in for her. This experience remains another of my professional regrets. I've often wondered what direction my career might have taken had I played that role. On the plus side, this disappointment did convince me to pursue my career with more professional dedication. Despite my film and television experience, I still felt I was lacking as an actress. I also knew that I still didn't have the self-confidence necessary to succeed in the business.

After I returned to New York I was introduced to Martin Leeds, who at the time was Vice President of Desilu. He had, in fact, organized the company for Lucile Ball and Desi Arnez and likewise had arranged the purchase of RKO Studios from Howard Hughes which then became Desilu Studios. Martin was a very kind and giving man and he encouraged me in my ambitions. It was with his support that I enrolled as a speech major at Hunter College — and he also arranged for an interview with the Actor's Studio, perhaps the foremost training ground for acting talent in North America.

> "Dolores's motivations were really very interesting. She was determined to be a success one way or another. And her determination always rested in the creative arts." (Martin Leeds, quoted in the German documentary *Diamonds in the Rough*, directed by Regina Goetze, 1997)

I prepared for my interview with one of the foremost dramatic coaches of the American Theatre, Stella Adler. I was very nervous, and Miss Adler did nothing to put me at ease. In fact, her mere presence was intimidating. However, I somehow passed my interview and began my dramatic studies under Miss Adler's stern but stimulating tutelage. My training with her proved to be a rigid learning experience. There was absolutely no nonsense with Miss Adler. In fact, as I began classes, I got the definite impression that she wasn't too fond of me. Perhaps that was because I was still working as a model, or perhaps she regarded my previous film work as conferring an unwelcome advantage over my fellow classmates. More likely, though, it was the way I was invariable dressed while attending classes. One of the perks from my modeling was that I often got to keep wardrobes — and most particularly shoes. My 4-1/2" foot size had represented such internationally renowned shoe designers as Charles Jourdan of France whose footwear usually sold for several hundred dollars a pair. Always very conscious of my appearance, I would customarily attend classes fashionably attired, and I suspect that because of this Miss Adler wasn't too convinced of my dedication to the acting profession. Perhaps this was because her most successful and renowned student was Marlon Brando — he of the torn T-shirt — who was never known for his sartorial elegance.

I must digress to offer a brief observation on Brando. While I have always placed a great deal of importance on proper speech and enunciation, I have never thought that Brando's speech got in the way of any of his performances. In fact, as evidenced in *A Streetcar Named Desire*, *On the Waterfront* and, I think most particularly, *The Wild One*, his unique vocal delivery added a truly definitive quality to each role. While I never met him, I retain only the highest respect for Brando as an innovator and one of the foremost actors of his generation.

I suppose it was inevitable that Miss Adler and I would soon have a confrontation. And, boy, did we ever! In typical Stella Adler fashion, she chose to humiliate me in front of the class. I was definitely hurt and probably went home and had a therapeutic cry. However, I was determined to show her that I was not so intimidated to the point of leaving her class because of the incident. I have never been a quitter, so I stormed back into her class the next day, determined to show her that she could not easily get the best of me. Miss Adler made some remark such as ". . . ah, I see you're

Stella Adler and Film Historian Alan Greenberg, when he interviewed her in 1988

back." My response was a defiant ". . . I paid my hard-earned money for my training here and I intend to stay and get all I can out of this class — unless of course you wish to give me a refund." I cannot recall exactly what she said, but it definitely had to do with the way I customarily dressed in elegant high heels when I came to class. This was in no way a deliberate flaunting of my own ego. It was simply the way I chose to present myself. I always liked to look my best. I still do. It came as a pleasant surprise then when I received a call in July of 2007 and subsequent letter from Film Historian, Alan Greenberg, who reported on an interview he had with Stella Adler on the occasion of the 1988 publication of her book on acting: ". . . Arguably, she was one of the greatest acting teachers ever in the United States, Marlon Brando being one of the many great actors she mentored. She had an alphabetical listing of her pupils and, when she got to Dolores Fuller's name, she was quite complimentary. She commented on how good an actress she was and, as everyone knows, thousands of students would audition for her class and only a few would be accepted. I believe Dolores did some singing and Stella was very impressed with her dedication and talent. She also commented that Dolores would make a fine teacher of acting and I believe she did this when she moved to Las Vegas (yes, this is quite true). Coming from arguably one of America's greatest acting teachers, this is indeed high praise." Indeed, totally unexpected and never even suspected for a moment.

My fellow classmates included names destined to become quite successful in show business — Rita Gam and Jane Meadows, for example. But it was Warren Beatty who went on to super stardom (Interestingly, about 1981, when Warren was at Paramount Studios shooting *Reds* (which won him a Directing Oscar), it is my understanding that he convinced Paramount to acquire *Glen or Glenda?* and release it on the midnight circuit. Warren had the idea that my movie would attract an audience similar to that of The Rocky Horror Picture Show. If this really was in his mind, I think he was mistaken. Both had their share of transvestism, but the appeal of the films was entirely different. In any event, *Glen or Glenda?* bombed out as a midnight marquee attraction. The prints were bought from Paramount by Wade Williams whose acquisition of the rights were richly rewarded.

I always suspected that Warren was favored with a little extra curricular instruction from Miss Adler, perhaps because he was so incredibly handsome and blessed with a special boyish charm that seemed to make women want to fondle him. Sure enough! On one occasion I accidentally walked in on Warren and Miss Adler in the cloak room where Warren was enthusiastically receiving some pointers on how to perform. Or was it the other way around? I had little opportunity to observe for they made such a hasty retreat from their closet rendezvous that I couldn't even be certain that I saw more than Warren helping his teacher on with her clothes to sally forth against the bitter cold of the New York winter. I kept this to myself and, happily, nothing was ever said about my accidental discovery. Fortunately, Miss Adler appeared to respect me even more from that point onward.

Before any students could graduate from the Actor's Studio, we were required to perform a 15-20 minute show before the public incorporating skills we had developed during classes in the service of any unique talent each of us believed we could illustrate most effectively, be it singing, dancing or acting. I managed to parlay all three skills into my act when I obtained a 3-week booking as a nightclub performer at one of the New York hotels. I sang a medley of songs made famous by Marlene Dietrich, such as "See What the Boys in the Back Room Will Have." This was the first time I'd ever soloed on stage as a singer and I thoroughly enjoyed the experience. I had been taking singing lessons for most of the preceding three years, so I was well prepared. Throughout my life I've never been afraid to study. When I graduated from the Actor's Studio in 1957, it was as if I'd been reborn. I was filled with a confidence I'd never experienced before. For that I will always be grateful to Miss Adler.

In 1956 I'd appeared in my next movie *The Opposite Sex* that starred June Allyson, and though I didn't receive screen credit, my being in the picture did pay other dividends. I remember that we shot on location in New York and that we didn't have dressing rooms. When it came time for wardrobe changes, we had to change in the back of a car. I felt that there should be a regular studio and so went scouting for a location. I found a building that was for sale that I felt would be perfect for a studio. I brought Martin Leeds back with me and he was immediately sold on the idea. Martin backed me all the way and told the producer that I deserved a nice commission for putting this together, so I ended up with a "finder's fee" of about $5,000.

This aside, I was becoming discouraged with my film work. I decided I wanted to broaden my acting horizons and believed the best way to accomplish this was by doing work on the stage. Besides, performing before a live audience during my nightclub act had been an exhilarating experience. I was eager to do more. Fortunately, my agent was able to connect me with the Red Barn Summer Theater in Westboro, Massachusetts. The Red Barn Theater no longer exists, but in its day it was a popular and fashionable place to go. It was a beautiful, spacious building that seated 600 people and the shows were sold out every night. Before final seating and during intermissions, the management created a wonderful social atmosphere for conversation and drinks. Because of my experience as a film actress, I was able to land the lead in a series of plays beginning with *Bus Stop*. I played the role of "Cherie," which was the part performed by Marilyn Monroe in the famous movie version. This would be my first important play so I wasn't going to step into the role unprepared. Before traveling to Westboro I worked on the part with a drama coach so that when I went onstage I'd be very familiar with the character I would be playing. I went over big in the part and was particularly pleased when the *Marlboro Daily Enterprise* wrote, "She is regarded as the most talented leading lady ever to appear at the Red Barn, which covers a period of 20 years." One of my fellow actors in the company paid me a curious kind of compliment on my "acting," saying, ". . . If it was your intent to arouse every man in the audience the way you delivered 'That Old Black Magic,' you certainly succeeded!" I confess that it *was* my intent. I sang and danced "That Old Black Magic," performing on top of a table — probably in the vein of a Las Vegas stripper without actually removing any article of clothing. Nudity was not necessary. What counts for impact is what your moves imply and how skillful you are in stimulating the erotic imagination of the male viewer. I believe that art is never excessive and in the art of sexual expression, as in all art, the power of suggestion is paramount.

I continued to play leads at the Red Barn in such plays as *Father Malachi's Miracle* and *Oh Men, Oh Women*, among others. In the play, *Oh Men, Oh Women*, which was not a musical, I decided to write three original songs because I felt that there were three places in the play where my character could best express emotions in song. Without consulting the producer, I proceeded to write the songs. Happily, our director and the producer loved them and agreed to let me use them in the play. It was immensely satisfying when my songs were well received by the Red Barn audience. I confess that song-writing was a talent I discovered by accident. When I was at the Actor's Studio, in preparation for my nightclub act I was paired with a fine piano accompanist, Dr. Leonard Copen. We were in a recording studio making some demos when, during a break, he asked me if I wanted to hear one of his original tunes. I loved his melody and, when he finished, I asked him to play it again. By the time he was through, I was singing the lyrics that somehow came to

Copy of an ad for *Bus Stop* run in the local paper.

me from out of nowhere, as they often do when I hear a melody that begs to be sung. Leonard was impressed and told me to quickly write them down. We became partners after that and everything we wrote we sold to publishers who paid us an advance of two or three hundred dollars. This was early in 1957. All my life, I have always loved music and singing, but fifty years ago I never dreamed that a songwriting career was in my future! My "experiment" at the Red Barn Theatre during the summer of 1957 was a step in the direction that ultimately became one of the most satisfying career moves of my life.

In a decidedly indirect manner, my songwriting career moved a step closer when, in the fall of 1957, Planetary Music Publishing Company decided to promote one of its songs that had just been recorded by Johnny Ray on Columbia. The song was called "Pink Sweater Angel" so Planetary's publicity department came up with a promo notion that was charateristic of the era by holding a "Pink Sweater Angel" contest. I dug out one of my many angora sweaters — of course I had a pink one — and went to the Planetary office on a lark. Here is what "The Cash Box" Music Magazine, issue of November 16, 1957 had to say when it ran photos of me with Dave Bernstein of Planetary: "What better way to promote its tune, judging from the winner, Miss Dolores Fuller, who topped thirty-nine other contestants. Above we see 'Pink Sweater Angel' on a deejay tour to promote the record." Altogether, "The Cash Box" ran no less than ten photos of me with New York area deejays: with Peter Tripp of WMGM; two photos with Jack Lacey of WINS; with Al Trilling of WNEW; with Mike Comita, also of WNEW; with Mitch Miller, who became a good friend and helped me promote my four Johnny Rivers songs which were recorded on

All ten photos featured in "The Cash Box."

my own deedee records; with Jerry Marshall of MGM; also with Joe Saccone of WMGM and with the great Martin Block of WNEW, perhaps the best-known deejay of the era from 1940 to 1960.

If I can make it there I can make it anywhere

Chapter Nine

Going back to 1955, when I first left Eddie and went to New York, I was introduced to two men who would figure prominently in my life. The head of the Producer's Studio in California, for whom I'd done some pre-Ed Wood pictures, had taken a liking to me and arranged for me to meet two of his friends when I arrived in New York. These were George Swetnick and Martin Leeds. The first, George Swetnick, wrote briefs for judges and had immense respect and influence in Brooklyn. Most people referred to him simply and affectionately as "the Judge."

The Judge was a wealthy and influential man in New York as well as Brooklyn. But what I personally felt was most important about the Judge was his generosity in helping people. He was a thoroughly good man who found people jobs and helped in so many other ways that he actually changed lives. It was not uncommon for us to go out to dinner or attend some social function and have people come up to him, shake his hand and even hug him to thank him for some act of kindness he had done for them. He was a very high-class gentleman with impeccable manners. Despite the fact that he was 17 years older than me, I almost immediately fell in love with him.

My very first night in New York as I was preparing for bed after a busy day, the Judge called me at the instigation of my Hollywood producer friend and invited me out to dinner. It was late and I was reluctant to go out again, but something told me to go. Perhaps it was destiny calling. I got dressed and joined him at a high-scale restaurant replete with a live band. The Judge was a very accomplished dancer and we enjoyed a wonderful evening. I am

I didn't leave his condo for three days!

not ashamed to admit that this very first night that we met, I went back home with him to the beautiful condo that he owned. We didn't leave his condo for three days. He was a popular man with the ladies and had many girlfriends. But after he met me, he stopped seeing his other lady friends and stayed loyal throughout our ten-year relationship. It wasn't long after this that the Judge asked me to marry him.

The Judge introduced me to N.Y. high society.

He owned an 8-story apartment building in Brooklyn and wanted to renovate the bottom two floors for our living quarters. I loved the Judge and would have married him, but a whirlwind of events including classes at Hunter College, study with Stella Adler, trips out of the country and back to California, complications in my personal life with a brilliant film executive, plus summer stock at the Red Barn Theatre conspired to keep us from deciding on a date. The Judge also had far more to do in any given day than there were hours to accomplish them. His professional obligations for most of the year kept him too occupied for him to leave New York. But even when we were apart, we always maintained close telephone contact for we had a great affection for one another. However, our marriage was repeatedly postponed.

Through the Judge I met many influential people. He was active in politics as head of the Democratic Party in Brooklyn. He was

John F. Kennedy's campaign manager in Brooklyn and I became his constant companion to many important social and political functions. Perhaps the most memorable event he took me to was the inauguration of Kennedy in 1960. I proudly accompanied the Judge as his lady and I still have my inaugural program book with my name stamped in gold on the cover. It was truly a gala occasion, attended by dignitaries and celebrities such as Frank Sinatra and Kennedy's brother-in-law, Peter Lawford, among so many, many others that I met and with some, maintained sustained friendships. During the time of the inaugural celebration the Judge was often tied up with political obligations, and so he asked Henry Kissinger if he would escort me to various functions in Washington. Kissinger performed the same service for the Judge three years later when we attended the inauguration of Lyndon Johnson following Kennedy's assassination. My memories of Mr. Kissinger (I don't ever remember calling him "Henry") are dominated by my recollection that his thick German accent made him difficult for me to understand, but that we developed a certain empathy upon discovering that we shared a Hungarian background. He was always very polite and accommodating during the hours we spent together and of course I enjoyed the constant stream of luminaries that paraded past us. However, I must confess that I have never understood why people regarded him with such awe. True, he used his knowledge of international politics to impress anyone who cared to endure his pedantic posturing, but I found him boring. One thing I have to say is that Kissinger never tried to hit on me, unlike another man high in visibility.

Around 1962 the Judge took me to a local private affair for high-powered politicians. Governor Nelson D. Rockefeller was there and, at the cocktail reception in a special party room, he spotted me. He came over and walked me right into a corner, putting his hand on the wall so that I couldn't get past him. Then he proceeded to "interview" me. Not that I minded being cornered by someone of his distinguished good looks and personal charisma. I was really turned on because I had recently had my song "Someone to Tell it To" recorded by Nat King Cole which seemed to impress the future Vice President and he urged me to tell him all about it. Actually, he was quite delightful, so interested in my accomplishment, and I know that relationship could have gone much further had I not been loyal to the Judge. Rockefeller was going through a divorce at the time and I must say that under different circumstances I probably would have responded in a more positive manner to his advances. But, several years into our relationship, I was devoted to the Judge who was there, observed Rockefeller with me in the corner of the room, but was so secure in our relationship that he was merely amused. We had a good laugh about it afterward because the Judge was a confirmed Democrat and of course "Rocky" was a life-long Republican. They knew each other, respected each other, but had few occasions to socialize. The Judge and I were constant companions and I enjoyed being in his company. We went to parties. We traveled. In fact, it was while we were on a short vacation at his home on Pine Island, Florida in the fall of 1959 that I was asked by the Little Theater in nearby Fort Myers to play the role of Lotus Blossom in their stage production of *Teahouse of the August Moon*. The play had been a smash hit on Broadway and was made into a 1956 film starring Marlon Brando and the great Japanese actress, Machiko Kyo. Because my schedule was somewhat uncertain, it was decided that I would be alternating the part with another actress. I had a lot of fun with this role — the exotic costuming and Oriental make-up was a stretch for me and made the experience a memorable one. But what I remember most was being coached on how to properly speak a few lines of dialogue in Japanese. Surprisingly, to this day I can still recite those lines, but they are the only Japanese I have ever learned.

Eventually I decided to move back to California to pursue my film career. Big mistake. During a moment of insanity, I found myself married to a smooth-talking character that I left very soon afterward.

Twelve years after we met, the Judge proposed again and I accepted. I had recently come out of that unhappy marriage and, of course, had never lost my feelings for the Judge. We planned a July 4 wedding date. But just three days before, on July 1, 1968 while playing golf, the Judge was stricken by a heart attack and died. He was only 62. This was a terrible loss, not just for me, but for all of the many people who had been touched by the Judge's support and generosity. I cried for weeks. It took me a long time to get over his death, and I still think about him every day.

Martin Leeds also was important in my life. I confess I was seeing him at the same time I was going with the Judge. I was never proud of this double life which came about without a conscious plan and I certainly do not recommend such a bifurcated path for anyone. Perhaps I was led astray through immaturity, yet I am grateful for the way my life was enriched both by my years with Martin and with my dear Judge. Martin, being with Desilu, was based in Hollywood and only flew East a couple times a month for a day or two. The Judge also kept a busy schedule, as did I, so it never was difficult to juggle these simultaneous romances. The truth is I loved both of these men. Martin was married, but his wife at that time was institutionalized with a mental disorder and so there really wasn't a relationship between them. He was also a very giving person and was always willing to help me with my career and even arranged to have my sons Don and Darrel brought to New York from California where they had been staying with their grandparents after my divorce from their father. Martin was an industry attorney and a firm believer in education, so he arranged to get my sons enrolled at Carterette, a prestigious private school in northern New Jersey. The boys would board at the school throughout the week and then would spend weekends at my penthouse apartment in Manhattan. Don and Darrel, I'm proud to say, always displayed self reliance even from these early years and would take the train from New Jersey into Manhattan's Pennsylvania Station and from there take the bus uptown to my penthouse. My sons never expressed any displeasure over my relationship with Martin. And he certainly was never resentful with the priority I gave them. It wasn't exactly a father/son(s) relationship, but there was a mutual respect and a deep caring between Martin and my sons. Martin was always very concerned for their welfare and especially their future and helped me make plans in that direction. Don dropped out of Carterette to complete secondary education in California before joining the army; while Darrel finished at Carterette, then entered San Fernando Valley State College, where he graduated with a degree in Business Administration. Martin eventually divorced and found a wonderful lady who was a fitting wife and partner for him until his death in 1999. She invited my husband, Philip, and me to attend his

This is my dear sister, Sylvia, with actor Hugh O'Brien, Martin Leeds and me when we attended a testimonial dinner for Perry Como at the Waldorf Astoria on March 26, 1957.

memorial service in Beverly Hills which was characterized by an outpouring of sincere testimonials from dozens of film industry professionals who rightly held him in high esteem.

Both of my sons enjoyed successful careers: Don as a plumbing contractor and Darrel in Las Vegas real estate. I'm equally proud of both of them. While they always received my love, support and encouragement, they really went out there and did it themselves. That was also true of my half-sister, Sylvia. Sylvia was eight years younger than me, but we were very close. She was a beautiful girl who excelled in swimming and exhibition dancing. We spent as much time together as our respective careers would allow. Sylvia traveled a lot with her swim team and throughout the world with dance troupes.

Eventually she found herself in Havana, Cuba, where she fell in love with Batista's next Ambassador to Norway, the charming Enrique Rousseau, who asked her to marry him. I visited her for three days in August of 1957 and found out immediately that something was not right. Sylvia was fearful about something she was unable to explain because it had to do with Cuban politics, which she did not understand. Sylvia was drinking and she pleaded with me to stay with her. I didn't want to leave her because, most unusual for me, I had a premonition that something terrible was going to happen. However, Martin Leeds had accompanied me on this trip and had to fly back on business. Martin demanded that I return with him. Despite my love for Martin, he could be very insistent and he literally had to drag me onto the plane kicking and screaming.

It was just a few days later that my worst fears came true. My beautiful sister was found shot to death in her room at the Hotel Nacional. It was "officially determined" that she had committed suicide, but I believe it is possible that was murdered. The rebel movement had begun in Cuba, and Sylvia's fiancé, Ricky Rousseau, was a political power in Batista's dictatorship. I believe she was killed by his enemies. In any event, I was inconsolable. Her body was returned to California by her fiancé for burial and once again Martin blocked my wishes and prevented me from attending my sister's funeral. Perhaps it was because he saw how distraught I had become and feared that I might have a breakdown — go "off the deep end," as they say. But I was terribly saddened by being denied the chance to say goodbye to Sylvia and I regretted even more not being there for her in Cuba when she needed me. Martin's role in all of this prevented me from ever being as close to him as I was to the Judge, even though I never stopped loving Martin. My sadness over Sylvia's death and the stinging knowledge that I'd never be able to speak with my sister again found expression in my lyrics for a song called "Someone to Tell It To," for which Jimmy Van Heusen wrote the music. Originally, I had written the music as well, but when I approached Jimmy about using my melody as a starting point for him to refine as so often was the custom with my co-writers, he told me, "Dolores, you've got very good music there, why don't you use it and take music credit yourself?" I responded with something like, "Jimmy, I like working with you and I'm sure the song will be better with your music." Jimmy loved my lyrics and agreed to do the music. I'm sure this was the right decision because the result comes very close to being my very best song. My dear friend Nat King Cole later sang it on Capitol Records.

Nat "King" Cole as I knew him. He was a sincere, good friend.

What good is a dream, a plan or a scheme
The rainbow that you pursue?
It's everything and it's nothing
Without someone to tell it to.

How eager you are to get to that star
But after the journey's through.
You're only a lonely dreamer
Without someone to tell it to.

There'll be blue days, hard-to-get-through days
Days when you just want to die.
Soon you're older, and the world's colder
When there's no shoulder to cry on.

Castles in air are empty and bare
With no one to share the view.
The moonlight is merely moonlight
There's no magic in I love you
Without someone, someone to tell it to.

Bad photo-booth shot of me and Jimmy van Heusen, but it's clear we were having fun.

Many people are surprised to discover that I had my own record company back in the late 1950s. In 1957 I started deedee Records, an enterprise financed by Martin Leeds and run by myself as talent manager and promoter. We made a good team. My photo in top hat and tights was on the 45 rpm label. We were especially fortunate to have a 17-year old singer named Johnny Rivers approach us for a recording contract. Johnny, whose actual surname was Ramistella, was talented, had his own distinctive style and we were happy to sign him to our label. Johnny was a nice kid, but definitely impatient. He wanted to get to the top quickly. I took him to Nashville where we recorded four songs on my deedee label, for

Johnny Rivers was good as his own agent even at 17 when I recorded his first four songs.

which I still own the rights.

We used musicians from Ricky Nelson's band, forming what was then called "The deedee Orchestra under the Direction of Irving Spice." Those four songs on my deedee label are now collectors' items: "Such a Fool For You," "That's My Babe," "Your First and Last Love" and his biggest hit of the four, "The White Cliffs of Dover." It wasn't long before his talents were recognized by others in the industry, soon leading to his signature song, "Secret Agent Man." At one point when I was in the hospital, Johnny came to see

Dancing up a storm on my own deedee label in 1958.

me. Apparently, Hank Williams' widow, Audrey, had also seen the potential in Johnny and wanted to buy out his contract. Johnny was a budding star, true, but this belief in his own potential also came across as an almost arrogant independence. He would fly in from Memphis to New York without telling Martin and me that he was coming and hand us the plane tickets and the hotel bill and tell us that he had booked himself on *The Dick Clark Show*. This sort of willful independence happened more than once. Obviously this was not the way to conduct a business association. I have always prided myself on possessing keen business acumen, and particularly a sharp eye for spotting talent. I was inclined to hang onto Johnny a while longer. But Martin felt that his extravagances were becoming a drain on our company's coffers and his willfulness required too much of our time, so he persuaded me to let Johnny out of his contract. I negotiated an excellent deal with Audrey and Martin was genuinely surprised that he got his entire investment back . . . with a little to spare, owing to residuals from sales of deedee records.

Audrey Williams wanted Johnny badly and offered him perks that we were not willing to match. We could nurture his talents and give him the right representation, but we simply wouldn't give him a new Cadillac to tool around in. Later I heard that Johnny's association with Audrey did not end on a happy note. Audrey had moved Johnny into her home, but he grew dissatisfied with the arrangement. I later heard stories from my friends, The Jordanaires, who often performed as Elvis Presley's background singers, that Johnny would call up crying, "Get me out of here!"

Two other singers on my deedee Record label were a nice-looking Italian boy whom I enjoyed working with and a girl I really wasn't able to do anything with. Neither made the impact of Johnny Rivers and not long after Johnny's departure, deedee Records dissolved and I ventured forward into new creative endeavors. It seemed that each of my experiences in the entertainment field, failed or otherwise, kept bringing me closer to where I was meant to be.

Me and the man I should have married.

At the time of "Teahouse" in Ft. Myers, Florida.

With a song in my heart
Chapter Ten

Because I was kept so busy with my record company, talent management, summer stock, traveling, spending winters in Florida with the Judge and songwriting, I began to realize by 1960 that my film career had been languishing. I had appeared in a bit part in the movie **The Opposite Sex**, but that was in 1956 — four years earlier. I was eager to get back into movies and was particularly excited when my agent told me about a small role upcoming in Elvis Presley's latest movie, **Blue Hawaii**, that he thought I would be right for. It so happened that the picture was being produced by my old boy friend, Hal Wallis, who was a leading motion picture producer at Warner Brothers, recently transplanted to Paramount and a very sexy man — certainly in my relationship with him. Hal and I had become close when I worked at Warner Brothers some five years earlier, so I felt I had an excellent chance for the part of the schoolteacher. Hal came into town and took me out to dinner and a movie. After that we went home to my penthouse apartment and I played for him some of the songs I'd been writing as well as those Johnny Rivers had recently recorded on my own label. Well, it was an evening that changed my life. Hal said to me: "Dolores, why do you want to be an actress when you write like this? You are now in your late 'thirties. You can't be an ingenue forever. I want you to work on my picture as a songwriter." I was flattered, but still wanted very much to get a part — any part — and go to Hawaii with Elvis. Thank Goodness that Hal was able to persuade me that songwriting could be a much more rewarding career. He arranged for me to meet with Freddie Bienstock two days later at Hill and Range Music. Bienstock was

RIGHT: **Elvis was always a perfect gentleman with me and writing songs for him has been one of the most rewarding experiences of my life.**

BELOW: **I am working on a song for Elvis.**

the fellow who published *all* the songs that went into the Presley pictures. He and Hal soon scheduled me to meet two gentlemen who were expert music writers, Ben Weisman and Fred Wise. Sadly, Fred was not with us for long. He discovered that his wife had been cheating on him and, one night when she was returning from a rendezvous — getting out of her car to enter their high-rise New York apartment building — Fred threw himself from the balcony and smash-landed dead at her feet. Ben was one of the top composers in the music field who wrote fifty-seven songs for Elvis — several with me — as well as hits for Barbra Streisand, Sammy Davis, Jr., Sarah Vaughn, Johnny Mathis, Dean Martin, Doris Day and Dinah Shore Our meeting clicked and together we wrote two songs for **Blue Hawaii**: "Steppin' Out of Line" (for which only the music was used, though Elvis later recorded it for RCA) and the hit song "Rock-a-Hula Baby" that hit the charts at #23 and stayed right up there for six months. The A-side of the record was "Can't Help Falling In Love" — also from **Blue Hawaii** — and a #1 hit. Once deejays began flipping the record over and playing "Rock-a-Hula Baby," the 45 became a double-sided hit, with "Rock-a-Hula Baby" eventually going to #3 and selling over a million copies. The **Blue Hawaii** soundtrack LP was another enormous hit, reaching #1 and staying on the charts for 79 weeks.

In Japan, "Rock-a-Hula Baby" sustained #1 position for many weeks and is remembered by a great many Japanese music fans of Elvis.

Chubby Checker's "The Twist" was the dance craze at the time, and to further promote the picture, Hal Wallis put up a banner that stretched across the whole theater front that read: **SEE ELVIS DO THE ROCK-A-HULA TWIST**, which was also nice publicity for our song. It was exciting to have a song I had written performed by Elvis Presley, and then to see it rocket to the top of the charts. I was grateful to Hal Wallis for talking me out of doing a tiny acting role in the picture for which I would have been paid a small amount for the shoot with no residuals and instead offering me the opportunity for a much more rewarding career. I still get good residuals for that song and had a wonderful time writing it with Ben and Fred. The superb professional judgement characteristic of Hal was reinforced when Film Historian Alan Greenberg wrote to me recently: "I met

Hal Wallis was a sexy friend who always was there to help me. Here he is with film historian Alan Greenberg a decade or two after we had drifted apart.

Hall Wallis during the mid-1960's and we spent a great deal of time together during his later life, meeting in the Palm Springs area for a series of interviews about his illustrious career. He was, I believe, the first independent film producer to sign Elvis Presley to a contract and we would watch Elvis films. I inquired about various composers he used for the films, since many of them were simply vehicles for Presley's songs. He pointed out that one of the best writers was actress Dolores Fuller, whom he had helped become a composer for some of the Elvis pictures. If I recall, he said she was trying out for a part in the film *Blue Hawaii*, when he suggested that she use her talents to get into song writing, as the rewards were greater and would last for a lifetime. He also said, since Dolores was both an actress and took ballet, that she had the ability to put those talents into a song, whereas the standard composer would not. He believed that she and her partner composed some of the best work for Presley." Coming as it did many years after my close personal relationship with Hal, I feel a particularly warm sense of gratitude for those recollections by one who meant so much to my life.

Not that writing for Elvis was without stress. The competition was fierce. Twelve of the top writing teams in the country received the scripts, and these included such names as Phil Spector and Mac Davis; Jerry Leiber and Mike Stoller. I was invited to join the team of Ben Weisman and Fred Wise and eventually replaced Fred What we usually did was to cut a "demo" of each song for about $600, with Ben producing and arranging and Glen Campbell singing. These demos helped Glen launch his career. All the demos would then be submitted to Hill and Range, with Freddie Bienstock, the picture's director, Elvis's manager, Colonel Tom Parker, and occasionally Elvis himself making the final selections. The "Colonel" — think Kentucky Fried Chicken instead of legitimate military rank — hated women and I always breathed a sign of relief when my male co-writers helped my work get past him. Film historian Alan Greenberg recently recalled an obscure incident that gave me a great deal of satisfaction. Writing in July of 2007, he recounted how he met Barbara Stanwyck through his very long association . . . "with the great director, Frank Capra. As many of you know, he is credited with giving her her break in films and they were very close. Barbara was starring with Elvis in the film **Roustabout**. She confided to me that she was not particularly thrilled with being in a Presley film as this was not exactly her type of co-star. One day on the set, she heard the song 'Big Love Big Heartache' and said, 'This is really good. Who wrote it?' We checked and of course the composer was Dolores Fuller and her partner (Ben Weisman). Ms. Stanwyck had a turn-about in her thinking and, if you view the film today, you can see how enthusiastic she is, not only about working with Elvis but participating as a carnival owner in the musical numbers . . . I thought this was quite a compliment to Ms. Fuller, coming from one of the greatest actresses, in my judgment . . ."

I believe one of the reasons we were successful was that I had the ability to put myself into the character and motivate the plot. My years of experience working behind the scenes of films and understanding what the director wanted — the emotional impact of the scene — that's what sometimes gave me a better understanding than many of the writing teams to motivate the plot and make my songs fit more logically into the movies and feel they belonged at

Ben was never one to lie down on the job. He was "my Gershwin"; I his "idea gal."

the point in the story where Elvis sang them. My working environment was also very important to my creativity. A lot of the songwriters who were under contract were being paid salaries of about $150 per week. They were put in a small room with a piano all day, where everything they wrote belonged to Hill and Range. I couldn't work that way. I had a spacious penthouse in New York and when I got a script, I took the phones off the hook so there would be no distractions and just went to work. Sometimes I would be alone in a creative mood and, at other times, my co-writers would join me and my Steinway to work on putting my words to music. Ben Weisman always referred to me as his "idea gal" and I still think of him as my George Gershwin. Very often I would come up with a rough melody for my words which Ben or my other co-writers would then refine and elaborate. *Alas!* Ben died on May 20 of 2008 — another of the treasured friends who have left me in recent years.

Unfortunately, I had many difficulties with Elvis's manager, Col. Tom Parker. He strongly resented having a woman on Elvis's songwriting team and it was only at Hal Wallis's insistence that I was allowed to compete. Parker was a harsh, manipulative man who thoroughly disliked having me or any woman around. He created a façade that served him well in his exploitation of Elvis. Not only was he no more a colonel than Colonel Sanders, he was not even born in this country but slipped in, an illegal immigrant from Holland. Parker has been given — perhaps it would be more accurate to say he seized — credit for Elvis's meteoric rise in the music industry. But it came at a cost. He controlled and manipulated almost every facet of Elvis's life, and Elvis, who was a simple country boy, both naïve and trusting, always went along with whatever the colonel said.

Elvis never acted like the huge star he truly was. He was funny, self-effacing, always polite and soft-spoken. The first time I met him was in an elevator in New York. He was going up to see Freddie Bienstock whose Hill and Range Music was situated in the Brill Building. I said, "Hi," to Elvis and he just returned the greeting because the elevator ride was short and there was no time for conversation. When we got off on our floor, I led Elvis over to the reception desk because it was the first time that he had been to Freddy's office. The receptionist was busy and never bothered to look up as we approached her desk. Elvis asked politely, "Is Mr. Bienstock in?" The girl still didn't look up when she asked, "Do you have an appointment?" Elvis replied, "No ma'am," Still half-concentrating on her work, she asked for his name. He replied "Elvis Presley," and the girl was so startled she dropped the telephone she was holding. She popped up like a Jill-in-the-box and could hardly wait to announce us.

Despite Colonel Parker's dislike for me, I went on to write a total of 12 songs for Elvis that were featured in his movies over the next decade. Hal Wallis or one of the producers would always invite me onto the set when Elvis was scheduled to shoot one of my numbers and that was a thrilling experience, affording me even more insight about what goes on behind the camera. Even though I was living in New York for the first three or four years that I wrote for Elvis, I spent a lot of time in Hollywood, and I got to know Elvis very well. Whenever he saw me on the set he would always come over to speak with me and once he took me to lunch in the studio commissary. I recall one memorable occasion when I was on the set sitting in a director's chair that Hal Wallis provided. I was watching Elvis perform a beach scene with a number of beautiful, bikini-clad girls dancing around him. When the scene was finished, Elvis came over to me and invited me to his house. "We're having a little get-together tonight. Would you like to come?" I was so impressed that he would walk away from all these gorgeous girls to come over and speak with me.

"If only we knew then what we know now" — that's a refrain that most of us can sing. It would have been so easy for me to have a variety of photos of myself with Elvis. I just was not thinking ahead and, even when we were photographed together, I never once thought to ask for a copy. My dear, dear friend, Gloria Pall, was a top model and cover girl in the 1950's when she was featured on more than fifty magazine covers. She was in *Jailhouse Rock* with Elvis and was often visited by "The King" just as I was during those interminable pauses between scenes that plague the shooting of most movies — except, of course, the making of most "B" pictures. It is more than possible that Elvis first saw her when she had her own TV show as "Voluptua." On one of those

Greetings from "the King" + I " Jailhouse Rock"
Gloria Pall

Here is "the King" with my beautiful friend, Gloria Pall, between camera set-ups for *Jailhouse Rock*. Moments like this make movie-making tedium better than bearable.

breaks in shooting when Elvis was visiting Gloria, someone captured a simply charming moment with the two of them chatting.

Quite often, Elvis would invite me to small parties he would have at his home in Bel Aire, an exclusive community just west of

Gloria and I celebrate.

Beverly Hills. He rarely had more than a dozen people at these gatherings, and that made it more intimate and gave us the chance to talk. After Elvis began appearing at the Las Vegas Hilton, Ben Weisman and I were usually invited to be his guests whenever he planned to sing one or more of our songs. We customarily drove up together from Los Angeles for opening night. Elvis always invited us backstage after he finished singing, then to a post-show get-together in his suite at the hotel with close friends and other celebrities who might be in attendance. At one of these early Hilton shows, Ben and I were seated in a semi-private booth with Cary Grant and his wife. It was the only occasion that I met and spoke with Cary, but because it was so private, it was exceedingly memorable. During the intermission and afterward, we had ample opportunity to speak with Cary. I recall being quite stage struck in the presence of such an eminent actor whose work I had so admired over the years. Cary came across as a super guy, down-to-earth, with enormous self-confidence and no need to impress anyone. By not appearing to take himself too seriously, he impressed everyone even more. He deflected questions about himself by asking Ben and me about other songs we had written for Elvis, what we had done and were now doing.

Later, I went to see Elvis in one of his last performances at the Las Vegas Hilton. I'd brought my son Darrel and daughter-in-law Linda to the show and it was one occasion when I couldn't see him after the show because he had to rest. This was not hard to understand after what I'd witnessed on the stage that night. He'd put on a great deal of weight with a puffiness that was almost grotesque. Worse, he was not always able to remember lyrics to songs he'd sung hundreds of times, frequently turning to his backup group to cue him in. In many ways he had just physically deteriorated, even though he still had that magnificent voice. For someone who knew Elvis in his prime, this was particularly disturbing. I remembered him years before as such an attractive man who kept himself in top physical condition. While he had a well-known fondness for fried chicken and peanut butter and banana sandwiches, he counterbalanced his cholesterol-laden diet with daily judo workouts. But somewhere along the way, probably because of his hectic and demanding work schedule, he became hooked on uppers and downers — much as had poor Judy Garland. This addiction and the overall neglect of his body finally robbed the music world of one of its most spectacular talents at the age of just 42. It is no secret, too, that Elvis hated most of the motion picture material that was handed to him by the Colonel. He truly wanted to be a success in films and his performances usually transcended the superficial dialog and silly plot that surrounded him. The Colonel had bad judgment when it came to movies. He shoved Elvis into one aesthetic disaster after another, demanding more and more money because he knew that, with Elvis singing, audiences would come. On more than one occasion, Elvis confided in me about how he felt being stuck with second rate dramatic material and stupid dialog.

I hope he wasn't just being polite when he complimented me on my songs as feeling right for the point in the plots where he was to sing them. In two or three of his many movies, Elvis had a chance to demonstrate genuine acting talent and he did this with taste and style. Critics point particularly to *Flaming Star*, directed by the brilliant Don Siegel, with whom I had worked briefly some years before. Certainly the director is the key ingredient in the complex recipe of any film and when Elvis had a director of Siegel's caliber — as he rarely did — he gave us a hint of what a truly wonderful movie star he might have become.

I'm pleased to think, however, that I am a small part of the Elvis legacy. My songs can be heard in *Kid Galahad* ("I Got Lucky"), *It Happened at the World's Fair* ("Beyond the Bend," which opens the movie), *Fun in Acapulco* ("You Can't Say No In Acapulco"), *Kissin' Cousins* ("Barefoot Ballad"), *Roustabout* ("Big Love, Big Heartache"), *Girl Happy* ("Do the Clam"), *Easy Come, Easy Go* ("I'll Take Love") and *Change of Habit* ("Have a Happy"). For the movie originally entitled *Raceway*, producer Joe Pasternak was so enthusiastic about the song I wrote called "Spinout" that he actually changed the title of the picture to fit my song! Thus *Spinout* became the title song of the movie and one of the best and most successful of my Elvis songs.

I had a special fondness for Joe Pasternak. He arranged it so that I could have a writing studio on the MGM lot where I could work on the music for *Raceway*, along with my co-writers Ben Weisman and, at the time, Sid Wayne. However, this generosity on Joe's part hardly endeared me to other teams of writers on the Elvis films because they had to do their work cooped up in a small office in New York. So they complained to the Colonel that I had an unfair advantage being on location where I could get ahead of them in learning of any late developments. Consequently, the Colonel — quite predictably — saw to it that the playing field was "leveled." I had to give up my studio on the lot and it really was a lot to give up. Our competitors were absolutely right because being on the lot where I was in a position to learn about everything that was happening propelled me miles ahead of the competition, not only with the movies Elvis was doing, but with song-writing opportunities relating to every movie on the MGM production slate. Still, I liked working off the lot and would sometimes join my partner, Ben Weisman, at his home in nearby Venice, California while working on songs. Joe Pasternak and I were great pals for many years and I had a standing invitation to come over to his beautiful house with a guest of my choice on Sundays where he enjoyed hosting afternoon outdoor cookouts. Many top celebrities and assorted movie folk would be there to enjoy games of tennis, swimming, pool and other recreations at the Pasternak estate.

I'm often asked which of the songs I wrote for the Elvis pictures is my favorite. That's a little like having to say which of your children is your favorite, but I would probably choose "Beyond the Bend" from *It Happened at the World's Fair*, a song which, ironically, almost didn't make it into the movie on two different occasions. In the original script, Elvis played a crop duster who loses his plane in a crap game. I was asked to write the lyrics for the opening song that Elvis would sing after he hitched a ride in the back of a farmer's wagon. The opening lyrics I composed were "Wheels, sing a happy song . . ." The producer liked my lyrics but later decided for script reasons to replace the opening scene for one in which Elvis was flying his crop duster. I really had to fight for that song. I was still living in New York, so I called by friend, Bob Prescott, who owned the Flying Tiger Line. It was mainly an air freight line, but there was usually room for two or three passengers, typically crew members or relatives. Whenever I wanted to go anywhere in the world, I would call Bob and often he would arrange to have me as his guest on the next available flight. That was probably the next best thing to having my own private plane at my disposal. Fortunately, on this particular occasion for *It Happened at the World's Fair*, there was a flight from Teterboro Airport in New Jersey (actually the closest airport to Manhattan) to Burbank that very night. so I got on the plane and flew out to the MGM Studios in Los Angeles. When I arrived at the airport early the next morning, I took a taxi to MGM in Culver City and asked to see the script changes. It was obvious to me that very little would be needed to make the song work. All I did was simply change one single word from "wheels" to "breeze." I met with the producer, Ted Richmond, and convinced him that the song could still work. When he got over his astonishment at seeing me the very next day after calling me in New York, he readily agreed and there was no need to write an entirely new opening number. Seeing the film today, I have to say that the change from Elvis hitch-hiking in a horse-drawn wagon to Elvis flying his biplane beside the highway strikes me as a far more interesting and dramatic way to open the movie. Given that it wasn't really Elvis in the plane flying beside the highway, the close-ups of Elvis in the cockpit in front of the blue screen worked perfectly and only those who focus on the tricks of film making could ever question the illusion of Elvis, the daring crop duster.

The second time the song almost failed to make it into the film was soon afterward in the fall of 1962 at the Radio Recorders Studio in Los Angeles. Only one day was available to record eight songs and the morning session took several hours to record three of them because each one required eight, nine and ten takes. It was 4:30 P.M. before the three were completed and the musicians and Elvis finally broke for lunch. They were back by 5:30 to record the last five and immediately ran into problems because Elvis didn't like one of the songs and a lot of fiddling had to be done before he would accept it. It must have been after ten at night before they got to "Beyond the Bend" and, thankfully, Elvis was happy with take number three. Another half hour and they were able to knock off for the night.

I had also written another song for *It Happened at the World's Fair* that did *not* make it into the picture. It was a lovely song called "I'll Touch a Star" that Elvis was to sing in the restaurant that is on top of the Space Needle in Seattle where the 1962 World's Fair took place. Again, script changes knocked out my song but later Terry Stafford heard it, fell in love with it and made a fine, sensitive recording of it that did well on the charts. Truth to tell, I wrote quite a few other songs intended for Elvis movies which were not selected by the decision makers, but the song writing game is like that — you win some and you lose some. The fun is in the writing but the money is in the breaks. I was pleased and honored when, in 1997, a CD came out with all twelve of my Elvis songs, including additional "takes." This CD was called "Elvis Sings Dolores Fuller."

Naturally, not everything I wrote during this time was for pictures. "Cindy, Cindy," for instance, was a song Elvis recorded on the RCA label in 1971. I was pleased to have my songs performed by some of the best talents in the industry, such as Peggy Lee, who recorded "Losers Weepers," I was also fortunate to collaborate with top songwriters of the day. Besides my frequent partner Ben

Sammy Fain was, in my opinion, one of the truly great song writers. I wish I had worked with him more often.

Weisman, I worked with Academy Award-winning composers Sammy Fain (with whom I wrote "How Can Anyone Keep from Singing," a fun song that was put into the *Mary Poppins* album and sung by the Do Re Mi Children's Chorus), Nelson Riddle ("Marriage on the Rocks"), Mark Barkan ("I'll Take Love" for the Elvis movie *Easy Come Easy Go*), and Jimmy Van Heusen ("Sad Eyed Baby" and "Someone To Tell It To"). Also, as mentioned earlier, I wrote all of the words sung by Nat "King" Cole for "Someone To Tell It To." Sammy Cahn bulled his way onto the song because he was working with Jimmy and persuaded Jimmy to let him write the introductory "Verse." But those words were never recorded. They were published in the sheet music and can be found there but, so far as I know, no one ever sung them on a record. Nevertheless, Sammy got a share of the royalties every time the song played because he shared the credit.

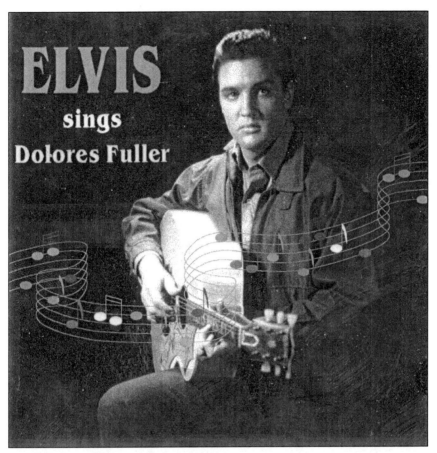

It makes me feel so proud that, of the 18 songs I wrote for Elvis, he sang 12 of them in his Hollywood movies.

It was customary in those days in the early 1960's for Nat and his beautiful girl friend to pick me up in his limo to have dinner with them at an elegant New York restaurant, often joined by Jack Gale, Nat's friend at Comet Music Corporation who published sheet music of his songs. (Jack is now retired and lives here in Las Vegas.) Afterward, we would go to the club where Nat was singing and where he invariably performed "Someone To Tell It To," followed by Nat having me take a bow. I have a vivid image of Nat sitting at my Steinway in my New York penthouse asking, "What else have you got for me, Dolores? Anything new?" I had two or three more songs that I wrote with Nat in mind, one of which he liked very much, but he never got around to recording it or any of them. He

Writer Mark Barkan worked with me for 6 months on the *Batman* project, still to be released.

was coughing a lot when he wasn't singing and, one evening when he was performing, he actually had to leave the stage because his could not stop his emphysema cough. That magnificent velvet voice was silenced in 1965 when the poor dear died of lung cancer. Nat was a true friend who left a legacy of song that will never die. Nat was a gentle soul with a spiritual side that he usually kept private. His father was a minister who must have had a great influence on his upbringing.

Another frequent co-writer was my son, Darrel. He showed a knack for songwriting at an early age, and by the time he was a teenager he'd helped me compose lyrics for a number of songs. A neighbor in California was head of BMI (Broadcast Music Inc.) who pressed me to write lyrics for the National Football League. The only hitch was that one could not, at that time, have songs registered both with BMI and ASCAP (American Society of Authors, Composers and Publishers), so I had to make a choice as to which organization to place subsequent compositions. I was a registered ASCAP Member but, since Darrell had helped me with some of the lyrics to "Spinout," "Kissin' Cousins" and "Have a Happy," I simply registered those songs with ASCAP in his name. Although I was primarily a lyricist, I often came up with the original melodic line for my co-writers, which they would then refine. That's why on some of my recordings, I receive the credit "Words and music by . . ." I believe that one can't really be a successful lyricist without hearing a melody in your head. I've always been able to do that.

Back to Hollywood
Chapter Eleven

I moved back to California in 1964 and bought a beautiful house on three acres of land at 8115 Mulholland Terrace in the Hollywood Hills. I always thought of it as a party house, and at the time I enjoyed hosting lavish affairs. I realized I had come a long way from my days with Ed Wood, whom I'd heard from my friend Mona McKinnon had married a woman who not only didn't try to curb Eddie's drinking, but encouraged it. There's little doubt that this is the reason he'd also faltered creatively. The dashing director I knew who had once pursued his dream with a boyish passion and who might have done better work if he'd had studio support was now an unkempt, bloated alcoholic eking out a living making porno pictures. It was so sad and such a waste of talent. But I didn't want any part of that lifestyle. I stayed away but have always regretted that I didn't at least take a shot at seeing if there was any way I might have been able to help Eddie when he was down and out, destitute and drinking.

Throughout my years in the entertainment industry, I was fortunate to have known many outstanding people in show business. Some I even dated: Frank Sinatra, Johnny Carson, George Raft, and producer Samuel Goldwyn Jr. were men I admired professionally and was attracted to romantically.

Frank Sinatra had been a big hit with the bobby-soxer crowd during the war years. He'd appeared alongside my dear Gene Kelly and other great song-and-dance performers in wonderful MGM musicals, such as **Anchors Aweigh** and **On the Town**. And then for some reason his career hit a snag. I knew Frank during this low point prior to his resurgence as an actor of substance and power,

Frank Sinatra and I had a brief romantic fling when he was skinny and younger.

thanks to his Academy Award-winning performance as the cocky Maggio in Fred Zinnemann's classic pre-World War II epic *From Here to Eternity*. The picture was made in 1953, so my brief association with Frank, if memory serves, must have come shortly after my first arrival in Hollywood when I was on the "Queen For A Day" show. He was short, he was skinny, and I didn't find him particularly attractive, but there is no denying the romantic quality of his voice.

My son, Darrel, began helping me to write songs when he was very young.

I certainly wasn't in awe of him, but Frank was fun to be with and I liked him. I don't know if he owned a home at that time. As I remember, when we would get together it was at a rather unpretentious hotel bungalow he was renting. But Frank Sinatra was really just a fling. I don't think we dated more than a few times. Certainly, he was not great in bed. Much later, about 1965, I had an opportunity to write a song which was to go into his movie *Marriage On The Rocks*. The producer wanted my song, but another of my unfortunate moments came when Frank, always contentious, quarreled with Jack Donohue, the director, and walked off the set before recording the song. That was disappointing, of course. Frank, singing one of my songs, would have been a wonderful feather in my cap. The film was a dog — no consolation.

Over time, I got to know all of Sinatra's so-called "Rat Pack": Dean Martin, Sammy Davis Jr. and Joey Bishop. The one I felt the most affection towards, however — though we were never really romantically involved — was Peter Lawford. I knew Peter for a long period of time in the early 60s before his good friend, Marilyn Monroe, died, and I spent many hours at his beach house in Santa Monica. We had a close relationship as friends and I fondly remember him hosting elegant dinner parties. There were more intimate moments with the two of us relaxing in his sauna. I don't recall that he was seeing anyone at the time. One night, after some steamy moments in his sauna, we came close to edging our relationship into the sexual. Peter almost persuaded me to go upstairs with him, but I respected that sweet man more as a friend and did not encourage the potential for anything more serious between us. After all, one member of the Rat Pack was enough. Sadly, after Peter was ousted from the Sinatra circle following JFK's decision (at brother Bobby's insistence) to stay at Bing Crosby's residence in Palm Springs rather than Sinatra's compound — for which Kennedy brother-in-law, Peter, was saddled with the unwelcome task of delivering the news — he drifted heavily into drugs and alcohol and died at the comparatively young age of 61.

Gangster-actor George Raft and I enjoyed a May-September love affair. His house in Coldwater Canyon was situated just below my home on Mulholland Terrace. We would frequently get together for dinner at his place where he'd installed a marvelous dance floor and we'd dance for hours. He always had a number of carefully selected records ready, which showed quite a bit of thought in advance. There were a few occasions when he hired a trio of musicians to provide live music for atmosphere and for dancing afterward. George, of course, was a fabulous dancer, smooth on his feet, although I must say that Ed Wood really was a much better dancer. George was always a complete gentleman, suave and considerate (contrary to his menacing screen image) and we enjoyed a two-year romance. George was well into his fifties by this time, almost twenty years older than me, but I was strongly attracted to him. George was a caring, generous person and was always on the lookout for ways to help me. On one occasion he took me to a top producer/friend at his private office on the studio lot, which was well appointed. We spent a very pleasant informal evening there. Nothing came of it, but this was an example of the consideration George showed toward his friends. I cared deeply for George and might well have married him. The problem we encountered was the

Peter Lawford was a sweet man and a good friend, but somehow I escaped his advances.

I fell in love with George Raft but his Catholic wife refused to give him a divorce.

same one that George's other girlfriends (including Norma Shearer and Betty Grable) had discovered. George had married back in the 1920s and his wife had never — nor would she ever — grant him a divorce. While she had been out of his life since the beginning of his Hollywood career, Grayce Mulrooney was still legally married to George. Seeing no future in furthering our relationship, we just drifted apart — although I still retain fond memories of our time together.

Samuel Goldwyn, Jr. was a very special man in my life. When he would fly in from California to New York where I was living in the early 1960's, he would often take me to the library or to a bookstore before we went out to dinner. Sam was highly educated and, since he knew how committed I was to improving myself, he would choose books that he felt would further my education. Some of the books that Sam recommended so impressed me that I bought copies to re-read and to have for reference in my library, so Sam really did have a vital influence on my development. For that, I will always be grateful. After dinner sometimes Sam would take me for a horse-drawn hansom cab ride in Central Park. It was a very romantic scenario. However, our romance didn't lead to anything permanent since ours was a bi-coastal relationship and I was still involved with the Judge and Martin Leeds. Yet we remained close. When I returned to California in 1964 and bought my house on Mulholland Terrace, I had a girlfriend named Peggy, an intelligent, talented writer who rented the two-story guesthouse on my three-acre property. I was fond of Peggy as I was of Sam and planned an intimate dinner party to introduce them. I can't remember now what fish I cooked for them — orange roughy, perhaps — or the wine I selected, although it may well have been Piesporter Goldthropfken Spalese, which I still enjoy. The dining room looked out on my flower-bedecked terrace, making a perfect backdrop for the flickering candlelight. They hit it off and Sam called me the next day quite incredulous to ask, "Is she for real?" "Yes, she certainly is!" I assured him. Sam saw more of Peggy, they decided to get married and, I'm happy to say, they're still together. Now, more than forty years later, we are still friends. Sam went on to produce some wonderful films and one of the best Academy Award shows for ABC television. His *Mystic Pizza* was the second most important film for Julia Roberts and, in effect, introduced her to the world; and *Master and Commander — The Far Side of the World* is only one of his recent triumphs. A recent issue of "Daily Variety" shows Sam still very active producing meaningful movies. One recent film, *The Whale and the Squid*, was in contention for Best Picture and other Academy Award nominations for 2005 The only down side to that dinner party was the inevitable loss of my tenant, Peggy. Replacing Peggy proved difficult. I was particular about my tenants and before I could find a suitable person to take in, an offer was made to buy my property that I accepted. Later, when Philip and I were married, Sam sent me a sweet telegram of congratulations in which he generously acknowledged that without me . . . "there would be no Sam and Peggy Goldwyn." Perhaps he had forgotten that George Cukor had him counsel Philip about the best way for his son, Francis, to prepare for a film career when Philip was an Academy Director. Looking back, it clearly was a mistake to sell my Mulholland mansion when Peggy left to marry Sam. Who knew during the mid-'sixties that property values would skyrocket the way they did? It wasn't long before the folly of selling that valuable three acres with such a beautiful home and guest house was obvious and triggered an interest in real estate that stayed with me for many years thereafter. Soon, I bought a motel just north of the Los Angeles International Airport in Inglewood, California, redecorated it and sold it for a modest profit. Next, I acquired an elegant apartment building at 320 West Alameda Avenue, not far from the Disney Studios that was somewhat run down. I devoted quite a bit of time to renovate it. My efforts were spurred on by having people compliment me on the décor of the rooms and lobby. The name of this building was the Delta Royale, nicknamed "The Bel Aire of Burbank." Was this a distraction from my acting career? Certainly. But I derived a great deal of satisfaction in learning principles of interior design and even more in discovering that I had talent in this field.

Later, about 1974, I was employed by William Oehler to execute the interior design of his new home on Augusta Drive in the Las Vegas Country Club. Much to my astonishment, when he reviewed my proposed renovation, he offered me fifty thousand dollars and amended my proposal to give me "carte blanche" to change or upgrade any aspect of my design that I felt would enhance the aesthetics or re-sale value of his home. "Bill" was then married to a fine lady who was terminally ill. On occasion, I would drop in to discuss one or another of my ideas for his Augusta Drive estate and I was extremely impressed with Bill's thoughtfulness and care for his wife. On one visit, I arrived just as Bill had finished preparing an elaborate dinner for her. The table was immaculately set, decorated with a fresh bouquet of flowers and lit with two beautiful candles. Bill insisted that I sit down and wait while he went into the bedroom and carried his wife out for the meal. He wanted her to hear the latest ideas I had for the estate because he knew she would be interested and he wanted to share the latest with her. When I finished, Bill had a surprise for me. He told me that he and his wife wanted me to move into his estate until I finished the renovation because they thought it would be more convenient for me until my job was completed. In addition, he gave me a $10,000 initial payment and told me that he was prepared to stretch the payments over a period of years if it would help me for tax reasons. This sort of thoughtfulness was typical of Bill's consideration, which was corroborated by accounts I heard from many others. I had bought a two-story condominium on the opposite side of the Golf Club to the north of the estate and pointed out to Bill that it was a relatively short commute. Whereupon, Bill suggested that I rent out the condo until the job was finished and make a little extra money while eliminating the commute. This, as Brando said in *The Godfather*, was an offer I couldn't refuse! Bill's wife died not long after this and it was clear that he wanted to make her final time on this

Not marrying Bill Oehler might have been the mistake that led to the Soggy mistakes.

earth as pleasant as he possibly could. Bill often took me to dinner and seemed to keep looking for things he could do for me, such as guiding my stock investments. He was an astute counsel in the market and his investment advice was almost always correct. After another year or two, Bill began asking me to marry him. I would have been wise to do so because his surpassing goodness was as infinite as it was rare. There were two problems: He was somewhat boring; and I was being romanced at the time by a classy real estate developer named Paul Barry Sogg.

Born March 17, 1900 in Cleveland, Ohio to Lithuanian Jewish immigrants Abraham and Sarah Sogolowitz, Paul had married Florence Altman in 1920 after serving in the U. S. Navy during World War I. This was a full three years before I was born! Paul looked far younger than his years (so did I), had fine taste, was well educated and well read. His custom-tailored wardrobe was extensive, extremely varied and this little man (five feet two inches) was rich. I am ashamed to admit that this last asset — and he certainly had a lot of assets — influenced me far too much. I had passed the age

Marrying Paul Sogg was a mistake. Marrying him a second time was a *huge* mistake.

of fifty and was beginning to value security. Why had I not learned that security is an illusion? But I had not learned, so on February 22, 1975 Paul and I were married and celebrated with a cruise. I loved to travel, but I noticed on board ship that whenever a man showed interest in me, however innocent or casual, Paul displayed jealousy and always over-reacted. I told myself that this was no doubt owing to his inferiority complex. I had reason to believe that he was bullied by larger boys when he was a kid and by his nine siblings. Also, I leaned that he was a "teacher's pet" so perhaps he was simply "spoiled rotten." In any event, from then on, I took pains to fend off male attention and do everything I could to make Paul feel secure in our marriage.

Soon, Paul took me on a trip to Israel. This was a wonderful experience for me because everything about the trip was first class . . . the air accommodations, the hotels where we stayed and the way the friendly Israelis treated us. Soon, though, I learned that Paul was a master manipulator and habitually held out carrots to curry favors and then find excuses to back out of oral agreements, frustrate expectations and get the better of everyone he came into contact with. He had made some very minor contributions to Israeli causes, always with the promise of much more to come. Leaders of these causes are still waiting.

I had developed severe back problems early in the 1960's, had to wear a brace, and finally was scheduled for a spinal fusion operation in 1962. But the night before surgery, I read in the newspaper how Jeff Chandler had died from a spinal fusion operation that had gone wrong. The very next morning, I checked myself out of the Los Angeles hospital and accepted the invitation of my friend, Elena da Vinci to accompany her to Cuernavaca, Mexico for injections of live embryonic cells. Elena was abreast of everything happening in Hollywood and had been trying to have me do what many Hollywood actresses were doing to stay young and attractive. Live embryonic therapy had been pioneered in Switzerland in the 1930's by Dr. Niehans, but this wonderful therapy had not yet been accepted in the USA. As of 2008, it still is not, even though this splendid practice works! Within a few weeks, I threw away my brace and was back on the golf course. Sad to say, live cells — unlike stem cells — are not a permanent cure. Thirteen years had passed from my first injections to my "Soggy" marriage and the old back problems were starting to return. Paul had known people who had been treated with live embryonic cells and readily agreed to take me to Heidelberg, Germany, where he knew of a distinguished student of Dr. Niehans, a Dr. Swartz, who once more helped me to overcome by back problems. He also treated Paul successfully. I appreciated Paul's support in this vital matter, but problems were beginning to plague our union. Paul forced me to stop my management of talent and devote my time to helping him. Then he forced me to sell my condo on the Golf Course, even though the rental income was helpful to me. It had made me somewhat independent and now I found that Paul wanted me to bring him the receipts from the grocery store and any other store so he could add the cost of whatever I bought to the change I had left over from the money he gave me for shopping. I began to realize that he was a control freak. I was grateful when he produced a movie, **Horace and Fred**, and had Ben Weisman and me write several songs for it. Of course, he got a much needed tax write-off for it so there was a quid pro quo. That was before the 1976 ruling ending tax write-offs for movies. What really turned the tide, however, was the realization that Paul loved his big boxer dogs more than he loved me. The dogs would snarl whenever I approached Paul and finally one of them chewed up my arm as I was serving dinner to Paul. This vicious attack resulted in twenty eight stitches and a mangled finger that still bothers me today. That did it. "Paul, either those dogs go or I go." The dogs didn't go, so on February 2, 1976 I went. It was a little less than one year from the time I walked down the aisle to the time I walked out. I didn't ask for alimony and took with me a watch and a $60,000 sable coat with my name embroidered inside — small compensation for the suffering. Bill Oehler reappeared, but I was not yet ready for another marriage. Life is an experiment in timing and my timing definitely was off.

Diamonds in the Rough
Chapter Twelve

In 1997 I was the subject of a German documentary directed by Regina Goetze that she called *Diamonds in the Rough*. The significance of that title is drawn from my lifelong skill in spotting unpolished talent which I would undertake to represent and polish for professionalism and public presentation. Johnny Rivers, of course, was my first major find in 1957, although his unpolished qualities were the heart of his charm. I worked with him and believe I helped him to become a star in the music industry. I had hoped to discover and nurture more talent through deedee Records, my record company, but was unable to generate the same industry interest that I'd had with Johnny. Perhaps this was because Johnny had a great deal of savvy about promoting himself and devoted a great deal of his energy toward this end.

Still, I found a particular satisfaction helping talented people succeed in their dreams. So in 1965, after I had relocated to California, I partnered with my friend Hank Levine to form Music Management with our office located on the Sunset Strip in Hollywood. The purpose of the company was not only to develop and manage music and recording artists, but also to arrange bookings for their acts in Las Vegas lounges and elsewhere. Hank's wife, the beautiful and talented Mariana, had studied dance and was featured with Eugene Loring's Dance Players, so we had a strong bond of common interest. Hank had a variety of interests and awesome talent in the music field as an arranger and conductor. Hank arranged for Ann-Margret, Opraland, Channel 5 and was so busy at one point that he actually turned down the opportunity early in Elvis Presley's career to produce Elvis Presley's recording

Hank Levine and I managed Charo until Cugat's continual interferance discouraged further efforts.

sessions, which Mariana has never let him forget. Through Music Management, we discovered a number of exceptional talents to showcase in top Las Vegas hotel lounge shows.

"The Country Affair" was a collection of very talented young people who could sing, dance and play instruments, but Hank Levine and I were not able to manage them to the top.

Will anyone today remember "The Country Affair" or "The Deltas"? These two groups had brief, promising moments in the sun but broke up before Hank and I could recoup our investments. Since it has always been important for singers and performers to know how to move, Mariana would choreograph our groups, which greatly enhanced their performances. One of our most successful acts was a group that Hank and I put together called "The Aristocracy." To build our talent roster we advertised in *Variety* and then auditioned those who responded and impressed us with their talent as musicians and with their singing and dancing skills. "The Aristocracy" consisted of six very talented young people — four men and two girls. We worked with them, honing their individual talents into a team effort and then began booking them into such Vegas hotels as the Flamingo, where the group often performed. I'm proud to say that our group performed so successfully in lounge shows that they eventually managed to secure a Warner Brothers recording contract. The leader of "The Aristocracy" was Mickey Elley, who went on to a successful music career in Nashville.

Hank Levine and I had better luck with "The Aristocracy," our most successful group. We got a Warner Brothers contract and lots of bookings. Their leader, Mickey Elley, went on to an independent career in Nashville.

It's interesting how "star potential" can often be stymied by the intervention of others. There was a now-famous singer-actress named Charo who sought our representation back in the 1960s. She was a cute gal with a certain unique style who, at the time, was married to one of the country's top bandleaders, Xavier Cugat, for whom Hank had done some impressive arranging. Charo also had an extraordinary history. She was born Maria Rosario Martinez Molina Baez. Her father was a lawyer who was exiled from Casablanca during the Franco dictatorship but who later returned after Franco died. Charo attended the Catholic Convent of the Sacred Heart, where she began playing guitar at the age of 9. Certainly Charo was a girl with abundant talent. At 14 she won a scholarship to study classical guitar with the world-renown Spanish teacher and performer, Andres Segovia. While her skills definitely placed her above the "diamond in the rough" category, she did require proper representation. Charo wanted to create her own show biz image and I felt certain that she had the potential. Since I had an "in" with producers such as Hal Wallis and Joe Pasternak, I arranged for movie studio interviews. These powerful men in the picture industry showed an interest in her talents — but each time before a deal could be made, the domineering Cugat (who was 41 years older than his bride) would insist that Charo go on tour with his band, thereby squelching the deal. Cugat had two tiny Chihuahua doggies. And once, at least, when she and "Coogie" boarded airplanes to fly somewhere, Charo smuggled them aboard, one in each pocket of her coat. We tried for as long as we could to get Charo parts in music revues and in films, but Cugat's influence soon proved too much to deal with, especially when we were working with so much other talent that needed developing, and we soon dissolved our contract. I took away nothing more than happy memories of the time I spent with Charo and one of the artistically talented Cugat's paintings. I didn't even get to keep that painting, which I loved and proudly hung on my living room wall, because another friend at the time, Buddy Hackett, literally took it off my wall and absconded with it. I should have made a big fuss and not let him get away with it, but that would have lost me my friendship with Buddy, which meant more to me at the time. Eventually, after Charo left us, she achieved temporary fringe success as the "Cuchi-Cuchi" girl on such late-night talk programs as *The Merv Griffin Show*" and as a Las Vegas entertainer. Now, in 2007, it appears that she has retained her charm, sexiness and appeal to Las Vegas audiences — something of a record, I'm happy to say.

Hank was increasingly in demand in Nashville studios during the mid-1960's and, for a time, was literally commuting between Hollywood and Nashville. Eventually, this sabotaged our partnership, although a major factor was an often-repeated pattern with our talent. We put money and time into their development and invariably something would happen to break up the groups. Finally, Hank and Mariana sold their lovely home near mine in the Hollywood Hills; sold their wonderful boat, "Bon Jour" (on which we would sail to

Semour Heller helped with Ronnie Fuller and especially with Elvis Presley, Jr.

I took Saymour to Windsor, Canada, to meet Elvis Aaron Presley, Jr. Here we are at "The Top Hat" club where Jr. often performed.

Catalina Island from Long Beach harbor), and moved to Nashville. At that point I became the sole owner of Music Management. It was around this time — 1966 — that I began my professional association with Seymour Heller, soon to become one of my dearest friends. Seymour was one of the best-known managers in the entertainment industry and helped me to fill the management void after Hank moved to Nashville. He was for a long time the manager of the Traniers although his most famous client was Liberace whose career Seymour devoted himself to for 28 years — until Liberace died. I found Seymour to be a man of honesty and integrity and we remained close until his passing in 2001.

Another fellow for whom I held high hopes was a singer named Virgil Gifford. I had seen him performing in a little nightclub in California and was immediately impressed by his talent. In fact, I was so certain of his potential that I paid for him to have surgery on his drooping eyelids which marred his otherwise fine appearance. Sadly, I managed Virgil only briefly because he became heavily hooked on alcohol and I reluctantly terminated his contract. Virgil's excesses pretty much ended his promising career and, eventually, his life.

On a happier note, about 1970 I became the manager of a real "diamond in the rough" whose name was Ronnie Beasaw, of northern Wisconsin Indian blood. He was brought to me by John Gregory, an eminent choreographer, actor and vocal coach because John was convinced that Ronnie had the right stuff to become a major star but needed professional guidance and my connections. After seeing and hearing Ronnie perform, I was even more convinced than John Gregory that Ronnie had the potential to become one of America's top music stars. Ronnie was a handsome boy with charisma and an impressive stage presence. I spent a good deal of time and money investing in his career. John Gregory and I shared responsibilities for a time and, since I was doing most of the work, by 1972 I became Ronnie's personal manager, devoting much of my waking hours for 3 years to further his career. I only wish that my efforts had been more effective during those years, but Ronnie worked hard on his own management, too, and showed considerable business acumen. A minor problem was that Ronnie had buck teeth so pronounced that he would hide them behind the microphone when

Ronnie Fuller, shown here with his group, was my talented friend whom I managed for a while from 1972 and whose career is finally in orbit in the music stratosphere worldwide.

he was singing. I arranged to have his dental work corrected through Elizabeth Taylor's dentist. I also helped him with hairstyle, wardrobe and learning songwriting fundamentals. Besides his onstage talents, Ronnie had exceptional abilities as a songwriter and so I encouraged his ambitions in that direction. We wrote songs together and Ronnie proved so talented that I took him to two of my co-writers Ben Weisman and Buddy Kaye. They, too, saw Ronnie's talents in composing lyrics as well as music and likewise were convinced that Ronnie would "make it big time," as the saying goes, so they spent a great deal of their valuable time helping to train Ronnie in the art of song writing. They were established and respected talents in the field, although I honestly believe that Ronnie had greater potential as an artist. One of my most valuable contacts was Billy Sherrill, the head of Columbia Records in Nashville. Billy was the writer of a number of hit songs and the guiding force behind a number of top country performers such as Tammy Wynette, Charlie Rich, Johnny Paycheck and George Jones. Through his hard work, extraordinary talent as an arranger and producer and dedication to developing talent, Billy earned his reputation as "King of the Recording Industry." Almost single-handedly, Billy redefined and broadened "the Nashville sound," reshaping it for consumption by a growing country music audience. I can't remember how I met Billy or why and how I became his friend, but I had worked with him both in songwriting and developing talent and developed a fondness that was equal to the great respect I had for him. Because Billy was the most important of my Nashville contacts, I took Ronnie to meet him late in 1971. Billy was very impressed, chiefly because Ronnie was — and still is — an electrifying presence onstage. But I had the notion that in those days Ronnie sounded a great deal like Elvis and possibly because of this, Billy chose not to put his considerable weight behind Ronnie. After all, Elvis was still alive and was "The King." There could only be one King. Ronnie remembers this trip differently. He recalls that during the two weeks we spent in Nashville he hung out with Billy, Clive Davis and Bobbie Wray because Billy heard his tape of a song he wrote called "That's My World." Billy said, "That's a hit," and wanted to record Ronnie's song and two or three others which would require Ronnie to come to Nashville. Ronnie liked Billy, Clive and Bobbie Wray. But Ronnie did not like Nashville, found it to be full of phony cowboys with hats, boots and western accents, no experience with cattle and music that Ronnie found full of cliches. Also, and perhaps chiefly for the virile young man he was at the time, Nashville women did not appeal to him at all. Ronnie actually turned down Billy's offer to stay in Nashville for the period of time necessary to complete a few record sessions. This may well have been the first and only time in Nashville history that anyone turned Billy Sherrill down! Ronnie opted to return to Las Vegas with me and continue a lifestyle here that appealed to him greatly. To me, his career then began what might be termed "a grand hesitation," so I will hesitate here and continue with his remarkable story later in this book.

Broken Dreams
Chapter Thirteen

Obviously, I've had my share of disappointments representing talent. But without question my greatest success during the 1970's and, paradoxically, my worst experience occurred when I took over the management of Tanya Tucker from a father who was unable to get her work or even to get record producers to listen to her. She was barely thirteen years old at the time. At a very young age, Tanya burned with a determination to pursue a singing career. The kid came from a family of humble means, and her father, Beau Tucker, actually quit his job to manage Tanya's career. Unfortunately, despite their travels to various record companies, producers and music people in New York, California and particularly Nashville, where they had hoped to hook up with Billy Sherrill, they met with no success. Only two things were clear at this point — Tanya's talent and her father's devotion to her. Some say it went much farther than that, citing the rumor that she slept with her father, but I feel this is unfair and not that exceptional for a closely-knit family of impoverished southern breeding and too few beds. Tanya's book "Nickel Dreams" came out in 1997. I got a copy inscribed, "To Dee — Miss you!" signed "Tanya." I eagerly read the book from cover to cover but was disappointed to see that she really *had* missed me, although not in the sense implied by her inscription. My name appeared nowhere among the multitudinous acknowledgments and, in the great many pages where it did appear, it was misspelled. Many, many of her facts were incorrect, reflecting many years of negative influence toward me by her father and less than perfect research by Patsi Bale Cox who "rode shotgun" on Tanya's admittedly bad road that was the writing of her book. Another factor that must be taken into consideration is the passage of time from 1972 — when I was able to get Billy Sherrill of Columbia Records to give Tanya a recording contract — and a quarter of a century later (1997), when her biography was published. A suspicious element in her book is the constant flow of quotations — literally thousands of them — by Tanya, her father, Billy Sherrill, Al Gallico, myself and others of remarks made a full twenty-five years after the events described. This and an almost complete lack of documentation must cast a very deep shadow of doubt on some of her story and, to me at least, on her perspective. Tanya was barely thirteen years of age when her father brought her to me. How many of us can recall precise details of conversations, thoughts and events when we were thirteen? I was forty-nine years of age at the time and deeply committed to Tanya owing to her unique talent and voice but, even so, I decided here to rely chiefly on my diary, letters and other documents to set the record straight about the facts relating to what made Tanya a star. I believe she wanted her biography to be accurate because throughout her book she shows remarkable honesty about herself and the kind of person her father was and is. How else account for revealing how her father made excuses to stay behind after I left the dinner table so he could take the tip money I left on the table? Stealing from a poor waitress! I could never imagine that kind of behavior by her mother, Juanita, who was a whole class above Beau. I liked Juanita and could sympathize with her because my first husband was somewhat like Beau in his attitude toward women. Tanya has to be admired for seeing the book through to the end. It is not easy to write a book, even for one who *is* a writer, as I have found.

When Tanya was thirty years old, the "Texas Tornado" was interviewed by Jesse Nash and George Flowers for the magazine "It's Hip." At that time, Tanya was only seventeen years from events she was asked to remember and there were far fewer errors. In her own words, tape recorded for the article, are her recollections in 1990 when she was asked to describe how her big break came about: "We were living in Las Vegas [actually in a trailer in nearby Henderson] and just doing every little show that we could . . . We'd already been to Nashville and didn't do any good there. It's kind of a funny story, really. We were all sitting on the floor because we didn't have any furniture and watching Elvis Presley movies and we saw on the credits the name of a lady that my Dad knew lived in Las Vegas, Dolores Fuller. He said, 'We ought to call her, but I'll bet you she's unlisted.' I said, 'Well, let's just look in the phone book and see. It may not be.' We looked in the phone book and she was listed and he called her. My Dad said, 'I want you to listen to some tapes that I've made of my little girl.' She said, 'Let's meet.' We met and she said, 'You need to be in Nashville.' We said, 'We've already been there.' She said, 'But I know a guy in Nashville that really needs to hear her, and that's Billy Sherrill at Columbia Records.' We didn't know who Billy Sherrill was; all we knew was he produced Tammy Wynette, George Jones, Johnny Paycheck — people like that."

Beau was Johnny on-the-spot and immediately came to my condo on the Las Vegas Country Club. He told me that he had heard I was as good a manager as Colonel Tom Parker, which was the kind of bull he threw to persuade me to take on the representation of his daughter. Regardless, when I heard Tanya perform and saw her intensity, I knew immediately that she had the talent to succeed in show business. From that day to this, I never entertained a single doubt about her talent. Although Tanya no longer draws audiences the way she did a few years ago and is usually relegated to second-class venues, her brother Don Tucker, for years her road manager, told me in July of 2007 that she is ". . . better than ever; absolutely fabulous in voice and delivery." I was happy to hear this and not at all surprised because few singers lose their voices when they are in their mid-forties. I still remember my satisfaction and excitement thirty-three years ago when Beau and I signed a document making me Tanya's first personal manager. Beau Tucker had to approve the signing of Tanya because she was a minor. Immediately I began to get on the phone with my close friend, Billy Sherrill in Nashville, to get him to listen to those rough tapes of Tanya. Billy responded to my entreaties with, "Dolores, what do you expect me to do with a thirteen-year-old girl?" I reminded Billy how Brenda Lee had been enormously popular as teen-age singer but was now getting older and I assured Billy that I was absolutely convinced Tanya would be able to replace Brenda in the teen market. Billy was most reluctant even to consider the possibility, but two facts worked in my favor: First, Billy was a true friend and respected my judgment. More relevant, perhaps, Billy loved to gamble and in those days often came to Las Vegas. It so happened that, soon after I began pestering him on the phone, he came with his wife and another of my friends, Al Gallico, head of Gallico Music Corp., to the Riviera Hotel on the Las Vegas strip. As usual, Billy called me when he hit town so I asked him to come over and listen to Tanya's tapes. But his first order of business was the Riviera's tables. I waited, fidgeting fitfully, while Billy built up a stack of chips.

In Vol. 17, #1 (1994) of "The Journal of Country Music" Tanya and I were interviewed for the cover story on Tanya by Daniel Cooper, who favored what Tanya told him, but the facts reported there were never contradicted. It is in complete agreement with an earlier one in the "Colorado Country Music Review" (Oct.-Nov, 1975) and with Tanya's interview for "It's Hip," quoted above. I called the Riviera and got Billy's wife, Charlene, asking her to bring Billy over. She replied that she couldn't do that because Billy was ". . . on a million dollar roll." I told her that I had a "million dollar baby" that was a far safer bet, but Charlene was not about to get in the middle at that point. The Riviera was a mere five-minute drive for me, so I went over and found Billy with a stack of chips that were steadily going down, down, down. The timing seemed right for me to say to Billy, "Why don't you quit while you're ahead?" After losing a few more chips, Billy did quit and, with Al's urging, we went to my condo, where I played Tanya's tapes. The tapes were not up to standard, having been cheaply made, but Tanya belted out the songs with professional assurance and impressed Billy and Al Gallico as she had impressed me. Billy told me ". . . the kid sounds kind of squirrely," but speculated that he might be able to ". . . polisher her up if she can work with me." He agreed to meet Tanya the next day, so we met at Katy's Coffee Shop in the Riviera for dinner. Billy arrived with Al and my friend, Bobby Vinton, who was singing at the Riviera showroom at the time and with whom I wrote a couple of songs. Thankfully, Tanya impressed Billy as mature for her age, and was receptive to Billy's comments during dinner, although Beau was ill-mannered and pushy. Billy told us that, if we would come to Nashville, he would sign Tanya to a Columbia Recording contract and rehearse her to cut two or three songs. Now all we had to do was get to Nashville. Beau absolutely insisted that he go with Tanya and me, which would almost double the amount of money I would have to front for the trip. I was not that flush at the time and had to find a way to raise the money since I wanted to avoid a conflict with Beau. I looked around for a way to finance the trip and, during a round of golf, a friend, golf pro John Von Neu, offered to help. In 1997, John saw appearances by Tanya on television to promote her biography, "Nickel Dreams," and was motivated to write an article in response. He called it, "A Star Is Born — Birth and Betrayal." Here are John's recollections of how Tanya came to sign a contract with Columbia and Billy Sherrill:

"During an evening discussing the problem (with Dolores and Beau Tucker), I volunteered to provide the necessary money. Beau was overcome with gratitude — vowed eternal appreciation. A promissory note was drawn with a proviso that repayment would be double the original loan [because] there was no guarantee that anything would come out of the trip. Many budding hopefuls had run aground in the Record Capitol."

We went to Nashville on John's money, but we didn't run aground. Before leaving, I took Tanya shopping for some presentable clothes and hair styling. I wanted her to make the best possible impression on Billy and those she would meet in Nashville because I was certain she could "make it." I booked two rooms for us at King of the Road, my favorite place to stay when in Nashville. Beau and Tanya took one of the rooms and I took the other. The next day, I took Tanya to meet with Billy and, true to his word, Billy signed her up with my approval as her manager. Photos of the three of us signing with Columbia were widely circulated and Tanya's father was not in any of the photos because Billy was just not comfortable with Beau around.

The next step was to prepare for the record session. Of course I had with me a song that I'd written for Tanya which Billy liked very much. It was called "I Love The Way He Loves Me" and was Billy's choice for the first side to record, but what would we do for the other? Billy gave us a stack of 78 rpm records from which to choose while he prepared for the recording session. Back in my room at

Bobby Vinton and me the night he met Tanya.

King of the Road, we listened to all of the songs and eventually returned to the Columbia office building to select two more to record with Billy. Approaching the front door with my arms full of those heavy 78 records, I paused for some help to get the door open. Beau just stood there. Finally, I asked him to open the door for me. I'll never forget his insensitive response: "No, Ma'am, I can't do that; someone might think we're goin' together." Somehow I refrained from assuring Beau that he was not the sort of man I would ever "go with." I can't remember what I did say; perhaps it was something about the need to pretend he was a gentleman, but finally he or Tanya or someone coming out of the building opened the door. Billy and I listened to several records from the few I had not eliminated and together we picked "Delta Dawn" and a third song whose title I have long since forgotten. Billy began rehearsing Tanya with just a piano. I still have a tape of that session which was never released anywhere. Tanya's brother requested a copy in March

John Von Neu and I subsidized Tanya's Nashville trip.

2006 and, since I've always been on good terms with Don — who has verified my statements in this book about Tanya and her father — I did not hesitate to agree to send it to him as soon as I could find it and make a copy, asking only that he not make commercial use of it because Billy Sherrill has never given me permission to let it out. That tape shows clearly the "squirrely," unrecordable voice Billy began with and his genius in extracting from a performer the best possible results. Without Billy's patience, extended to Tanya as a favor to me, Tanya would never have had a releasable record of "Delta Dawn" and possibly would never have made it as a singer of consequence.

When Billy got the musicians together and the session set up, we prepared to record Tanya. Then we encountered a problem that threatened to "blow the whole deal." As the session began, Tanya's

Billy Sherril, Tanya Tucker and me, her first personal manager, signing her to a Columbia contract.

father was at her side, holding her hand, perhaps to provide reassurance — which the self-confident girl hardly needed — or perhaps it was Beau's usual determination to exert as much control as possible. Billy was so exasperated he was ready to call it quits. He took me aside and said something like, ". . . Get Beau out of here! I can't work with the kid when he's in the middle like that!" I had been looking forward to that session but I put my disappointment aside and managed to persuade Beau that we should leave Tanya alone with Billy and the musicians so there would be no distraction. Hank Levine happened to attend that session and, in August of 2007, corroborated my version of why I had to take Beau with me out of the session. The recording went well and Billy and I began to prepare for promotion of the record with "I Love The Way He Loves Me" on one side and "Delta Dawn" on the other. Beau blamed me for taking him out of the session, but Hank confirms that it was at Billy's insistence. Certainly, there is no dispute that the results of that recording session were beyond all expectations. Billy must be thanked for that and Tanya does give him all of the

I tried to present her as a little lady as my photo session shows.

credit. In "Nickel Dreams," she does not even remember — or deliberately chose not to mention — "I Love The Way He Loves Me."

The first order of business, I thought, was to arrange a photo shoot. Billy set it up with one of the finest photographers in Nashville and even promised me to pay the portrait photographer, although it was not his custom to do this for his Columbia recording talent.

I took good advantage of the preparations made before we left Las Vegas, and the results, shown above, give the impression of a sweet, refined young lady. Perhaps her father disliked this image and perhaps, judging by subsequent indications, Tanya herself came to dislike it, but both Billy and I felt it was the right one for the ambitious promotion and publicity we had planned for Tanya and her record. Far from trying to make Tanya look cheap and sexy, I wanted an image of a young lady with taste; who could be respected and be seen as appealing which, underneath, Tanya really was. I have always felt that photos should be expressive of a performer's talent and personality so audiences would not be misled. With good photos, we then began a promotional campaign that Billy and I mapped out and copies of the record were sent out to deejays far and wide.

The next order of business was to promote Tanya nationwide. Billy liked my proposal to try to get Buddy Lee to handle her bookings because Buddy had built what was widely regarded as the most powerful agency in Nashville with the finest contacts coast to coast. I put a lot of thought into the best way to approach Buddy and decided that a carefully written letter enclosing photos and a personal follow-up would be best. Billy agreed. My letter to Buddy Lee included the following paragraph: "This bright, intelligent thirteen year old is already a lovely young lady with a beautiful personality to attract all who come in contact with her. Tanya can perform on stage as well as on records and has the potential of becoming a fine actress. Dancing is also an accomplishment . . ." I had begun dancing lessons for Tanya so her on-stage movements would be more graceful. She was "an extremely apt pupil," as the expression goes.

Much of this valuable training was acquired via the opportunities in performing with an older sister who at one time was Miss Country Music. Tanya was in school, but would be out and available for personal appearances on June 8, 1972. Much to my delight, Buddy Lee agreed and preliminary plans were quickly made to utilize both Buddy's Los Angeles contacts and mine. Always wishing to get the best possible representation for Tanya, I called Seymour Heller to ask if he would help me with Tanya's management as he had helped with management of the groups that Hank and I put together. Seymour agreed and we geared up for the string of top bookings we were sure Buddy Lee would quickly generate. However, things were moving much too fast for Beau and, as before, he insisted on going with us. I had been on the phone with the Los Angeles contacts almost constantly and knew that the deejays wanted to interview me and Tanya without the kind of distraction that Beau had given Billy Sherrill during the Nashville recording session. It was not easy to get Beau to understand why Tanya and I had to go alone. In "Nickel Dreams" Tanya accuses me of "really saying" that I ". . . thought they [her parents] were a couple of interfering hicks." This absolutely was not what I was thinking. Juanita never indicated that she wanted to go with us to Los Angeles and she surely never gave me the impression that she was one to interfere. And while Beau certainly was and often has been an interfering hick, that fact was entirely beside the point. A deejay's booth is already crowded with two guests. Even if there was no crowding, what could Beau possibly add to a radio interview with Tanya? I don't know if Billy communicated a warning to the Los Angeles deejays or if word got to them from Las Vegas deejays who were thoroughly repelled by Beau's crude and rude intrusions following the offensive way he elbowed his way through interviews that I had set up on our return to Las Vegas from Nashville; I only knew that the Los Angeles deejays had made it clear to me that they did not want him in their booths. I had come from humble beginnings myself, but I was never a bully and the deejays found much to discuss with me because of my Elvis songs. Sadly, this was the final straw with Beau and me. Already resentful of me and perhaps beginning to feel that my affection for Tanya coupled with a growing role in her life might encroach on his domination of the kid, Beau decided to get rid of me. Admittedly, this is conjecture. I'll never know what took place in his mind to justify the betrayal, but it certainly was not in Tanya's best interest to drop me as her personal manager which the subsequent, immediate downturn in her career proved.

Tanya and I took off for Los Angeles with a few copies of her record and stayed at the home of another of my close friends, Ted Tickton. At the time, I had an apartment at my disposal whenever I came to town that Ted had built for me by converting a garage on his Beverly Hills property separated by a few yards from his lovely home. However, Ted had no other guests at the time, so he had us stay in two rooms on the second floor of his big home. We were there only for three days because Tanya was not yet on her summer vacation from school. We took advantage of Ted's swimming pool which Tanya loved. I'd always been fond of swimming and felt particularly close to Tanya when we enjoyed Ted's large pool together. We were in town on business, though, and could only swim during breaks in a busy schedule. First we saw Chris Lane who interviewed Tanya for fifty-five syndicated stations. Bob Kingsley, Program Director of KBBQ, interviewed Tanya and me live on the air and played both "Delta Dawn" and "I Love The Way He Loves Me."

Also, we spoke with Bill Thompson of KBBQ. We were interviewed by Don Hinsen and Joe Farguson of KFOX and spoke with Bill Wamsley, their Program Director. The next day, Saturday, Tanya was interviewed by Russ Palmer and Larry Van Nuys on KCIL who were highly enthusiastic and predicted that the two-sided record would be a smash hit. We visited KMPC and spoke with Ailene McKenny who arranged for their deejay, Gary Owens, to play the record we left with her. Early that Saturday afternoon, we had lunch with Don Ovans of Billboard Magazine and then were interviewed by Bill Ward, Program Director of KLAC. All of this was duly reported to Billy by telephone who, though we were ". . . doin' great," wanted to discuss a possible problem he felt must be addressed immediately. It seems that teenage reaction to "I Love The Way He Loves Me" had been somewhat more enthusiastic than we had anticipated and deejays were giving it as much attention as "Delta Dawn." Billy felt that with a new talent, we could not afford to have a two-sided hit because it would split airplay. Billy felt that "Delta Dawn" was stronger and should lead our promotional efforts. I had to agree. Also, my song was less suitable for Tanya and less unique in the music field. We agreed to provide deejays with recordings that had "Delta Dawn" on both sides but to continue sales to the public with my song on the back. This enabled me to make good money on record sales, perhaps even more than my song might have earned me if it were released with something other than "Delta Dawn" on the other side. Today, my copy of the 78 recording with my song on the back sung by Tanya has become a collectors' item and also is featured in video copies of *Diamonds In The Rough — The Three Careers of Dolores Fuller*, which ran on German television twice in 1997. The English language version of this video is another collectors' item.

Most important during that Los Angeles trip, we met with Jimmy Saphier, a friend for twenty years since I had first appeared on the Bob Hope show. While sitting in Jimmy's waiting room, Tanya removed her new shoes and much to my alarm began scratching her feet. When I spoke to her about the need to get her shoes on as quickly as possible, she complained, "Mah feet itch!" Tanya put her shoes back on for the interview with Jimmy, but she never forgot the incident and, in her book, she blamed her itching feet on how uncomfortable she felt around me! No psychiatrist or medical doctor has been able to explain to me why anyone would get itchy feet owing to nervous reaction to the presence of someone around her. If true, this psychosomatic phenomenon may be yet another unique characteristic of that extraordinary thirteen-year-old. Nonetheless, itchy feet or not, Jimmy booked Tanya on the Bob Hope show. Also, Jimmy wrote to me afterward that he could get her on the Lawrence Welk show where she would get to perform "Delta Dawn" in prime time — one of the top television shows of the 1970's. Welk's music was a far cry from country but, thanks to Billy Sherrill, country was beginning to reach a much wider public than it ever had before and Welk was always ready to cast a wider net, according to Jimmy. Jimmy heard Tanya sing "Delta Dawn" live along with an instrumental tape that Billy Sherrill had given us precisely for such occasions and was thoroughly convinced it was much more unique than another version he heard, one of the reasons he booked her.

Before leaving Los Angeles, I sent by special messenger (for a mere two dollars in those days) a copy of Tanya's record to my dear friend, Johnny Carson, with a note about having Tanya on his "Tonight Show." I was dating Johnny at that time, a rather long-term relationship that had begun after being on his show some years before. Johnny's special quality of boyish naughtiness was to me absolutely irresistible.

Johnny came to Las Vegas often and invariably called me to come to his hotel suite (later his Vegas home) for dinner. Johnny often played tennis, stayed fit with a variety of exercise equipment (which would have me panting in a vain attempt to keep up with him). Johnny may have sent millions of Americans to bed with smiles on their faces but there were many nights when he put me to bed with a great big happy grin on my face. Despite this, I had determined never to trade on our relationship, so I stressed in my all-business note to Johnny when I sent him Tanya's recording that his decision to have or not to have Tanya must be based entirely on what he heard. Johnny called me immediately, enthusiastic about having Tanya sing "Delta Dawn" on his show and this validated once more my belief in the talent of a kid that I had begun to feel was the daughter I had always wanted but never had. Apparently Tanya has

Johnny loved this photo of me and each of us had happy grins from our often-renewed affair.

forgotten that preparations in Los Angeles for her promotional tour involved some dental work which I paid for. This is but one of many points in her book where she implies or states things that tend to denigrate me. I dearly loved the kid, so her treatment of me over the years, mostly due to her father's dislike of me, hurt me deeply. Not only did I take her to Elizabeth Taylor's dentist, as I had Ronnie Fuller before her, but I got her some decent clothes so she would make the best possible appearance. Additionally, I had begun to have her coached in dance so she would move more gracefully at

After a date with Johnny, I usually went to sleep with a happy smile.

the microphone. Was it a mistake to try to have such a young girl appear to have some class? Certainly I had no intention to demean her family background — remembering my own humble beginnings during the great Depression — but to prepare her for a career in front of widely varying audiences. My efforts were interpreted by her father as pushing Tanya to be sexy and flirt with the deejays. Absolutely not! One look at the photo shoot I arranged in Nashville for this child refutes these unfair assertions because these photos graphically illustrate the image that I had in mind for Tanya, an image of classy restraint appropriate for a thirteen-year-old.

Meanwhile, Seymour Heller made arrangements to have Tanya on Liberace's show — yet another opportunity for Tanya to have major exposure on national television. Seymour was Liberace's manager, so that was a slam dunk for him. But few of these arrangements were ever to materialize. In a phone conversation with Beau Tucker, I was told, "Dolores, we don't need you anymore." Returning home, I found a letter from John Manzonie, Attorney at Law, dated May 30, 1972 with this shocking message: "This is to advise you that Tanya Tucker is a minor and did not understand the nature of the agreement she was signing and, therefore, she disavows and disaffirms any obligations that might be imposed on her to perform for you in any manner whatsoever. As far as Tanya Tucker is concerned, she regards your contract as null and void and does not intend to be bound by any of the provisions thereof." Ouch! I put in a call to Billy Sherrill with the news. Billy was outraged, saying that he intended to drop Tanya from Columbia because, if Beau and Tanya no longer needed me after all I had done for Tanya, then he did not need them. I argued that Billy, too, had invested a great deal of time, energy and money in Tanya, that she did not understand how her father had manipulated her and that Billy should do what was best for his own interest and for the best interest of Columbia Records. Shortly after this phone conversation, I followed up on June 8, 1972 with a letter to Billy ". . . consulting not only with my own attorney but also with Howard Thayler, President of the Conference of Personal Managers, it has become advisable for me to institute a law suit against John Kelly, now acting as Tanya's manager. The suit will be for instigating breach of contract and we intend to file a lien against income for things that I have made happen for her. I don't want to cause any hardship for Tanya, but she should be made to realize that people aren't to be used and then abandoned." One of the first bookings for Tanya was at Lake Tahoe. Seymour Heller took it upon himself to pay Tanya and her father a visit to make them realize what a terrible mistake they were making. It was a long trip for Seymour from Los Angeles to Tahoe, but his professionalism was truly expressed in the time and effort he volunteered to take on my behalf. Had he been successful in this effort, it would have been beneficial to him, to Tanya and to me. Seymour was filmed for German Television in 1997 stating that ". . . Beau Tucker had seen the lucrative side of our management business, wanted to take over management of his daughter himself and nothing I could say would persuade him to be loyal." In fact, Tanya became Beau's meal ticket, once she got past Beau's blundering setbacks of mid-1972 to 1975 and her money has supported her family ever since. But without

Beau's bumbling by failing to have Tanya keep her bookings on Johnny Carson's "Tonight Show," the Bob Hope show, Lawrence Welk, and others (Seymour cancelled her appearance on the Liberace show), Tanya's career would have taken off like a rocket and she would have made her first million long before her sixteenth birthday. Her book "Nickel Dreams" takes liberties with the chronology of her career launch and makes it appear that Beau and Juanita fired me after taking one look at Tanya's feet! Not so. Beau engineered the switch to John Kelly while I was with Tanya in Los Angeles as the above quoted documents show. According to Tanya's book "Nickel Dreams," her Dad ". . . believed John Kelly's booking expertise could help. The first thing John did was release Buddy Lee as my booking agent and sign me with his own company, Artist Talent, in Las Vegas" ("Nickel Dreams," p. 85). This was a mistake that Tanya didn't take long to discover. Perhaps it was inevitable and only a matter of time before Beau would have found a way to resume control of his daughter's career. And Tanya's position in her biography that my "Hollywood glitz" was incompatible with the person she was, as she put it. Jon Von Neu's article reports on the developments at this point: " Returning to Las Vegas, we learned that another manager had lured Beau with advance money to take over the management of Tanya. We rushed back to the trailer home of the Tuckers in Henderson and pleaded to undo the apparent betrayal. But Beau claimed the commitment couldn't be revoked. The desperate need of money had forced the double cross of Dolores . . . Friends in the business felt Dolores had been badly treated. Billy Sherrill thought the situation was shameful . . . One added bit of duplicity involved my calling in the terms of the promissory note that Beau had signed with such flourishing gratitude. The part that promised repayment of double the money advanced was ignored. It even cost me legal fees to recover the principal amount. So now, how shabby it seems when one see the Tanya Tucker of today appearing on talk shows and in a biographical recounting of fame and fortune vividly portrayed in the showing of her Nashville mansion" (June 20, 1997 — written in response to television appearances for promotion of "Nickel Dreams"). Even Billy Sherrill and her Columbia Record Contract were dumped when Beau and Tanya had a chance to sign with MCA for a million and a half dollars. Billy was never given the chance to negotiate a new contract. At least not until the Tuckers realized the MCA deal was a mistake. So much for honor, integrity and loyalty.

If I may be permitted here to indulge in a bit of amateur psychologizing, I think that Tanya eventually began to feel guilty about the way I was dropped and to rationalize her way out of it by finding justification for the shameful way I was treated by her father. That is the only way I can account for the tone of her remarks about me in her book. After all, I had taken her on when she had barely reached her thirteenth birthday. Over the next two dozen years, her father, who disliked me and violated the contract they both signed in making me her first Personal Manager, never missed a chance to demean me and intercept phone calls and correspondence. On two different occasions after 1990, I sent demo tapes of a song I wrote for Tanya and enclosed heartfelt letters. I believe the song was exactly right for her, an opinion confirmed by the many who have heard it. But Tanya never responded, never so much as had her secretary return the tape with a reason why she was not interested. Perhaps Beau intercepted the tapes and blocked my access to her. On two occasions when I ran into Tanya during the Country Music Awards in Nashville, she was friendly and once even responded to my greeting with, "Hi, Dolores. I owe you, gal!" That response made me very happy because I have only wanted the best for Tanya and, if I couldn't remain her manager, I wanted very much to be a friend because I cared for her. But Beau remained hostile through the years, perhaps because he, too, disliked the feelings of guilt over the shameful way he treated me. Perhaps his hostility toward me was his way of running away from his feeling of guilt. This is the most generous way I can find to explain Beau, but it is possible, I suppose, that he is just a mean spirited, greedy person. His "We don't need you anymore" will always ring in my ears and that recollection will always hurt. Certainly we are very different people and perhaps I was not able to hide my distaste of his character behind a friendly smile. I accepted the inevitability of my forced leaving of Tanya over thirty years ago, but have always regretted that we could not remain friends. The way she has adopted her father's posture toward me in her biography is the final hurt. To her inscription in my copy of her book — "Miss ya!" — I can only respond, "I'll always miss you, Tanya. Call me sometime!" That would help heal the hurt I feel. The Monday, July 18, 2005 issue of **Daily Variety** headlined the news that "TLC goes country with **Tuckerville**," explaining that, "**Tuckerville** follows country music star Tanya Tucker as she attempts to make a career comeback while running a household as a single mom." The article claims that the new program has a green-light for 26 episodes of a reality series. When I read this report in **Daily Variety**, I fervently hoped that this series would indeed help Tanya make a career comeback and often think how her brother, Don, recently assured me that Tanya sounds great, perhaps better than she ever has. I planned to be watching that series and pulling for her but, on October 29, I received calls from friends who were watching the show with the depressing news that the show came across as a failed ego trip with the slim, attractive girl with the big voice now gone to seed as a fat matron showing off her Nashville mansion ablaze with light. Two of my friends reported that the dramatic high point of the show was her daughter sneaking into a Nashville night club against orders, taking the stage to sing with a second-rate group and being reported to Tanya — all of this so-called "reality show" replete with tasteless vulgarities of language and behavior. When I got these reports, I wanted to cry. If true, the show is doomed to have a short life and not be renewed, which is no way for Tanya's career to be revived. Not all of the talent I've managed have broken my dreams, as demonstrated by more than thirty years of friendship with Ronnie Fuller. No, my lifelong inclination to help people was not killed by the Tuckers' treason and ingratitude.

Even if the wound was deep, it was not a fatal wound and shortly after Tanya turned on me, I brought two other talented teen-agers to Billy Sherrill; the first of these was an attractive youngster named Brenda Smith. Billy signed her to Columbia and recorded her with "A Place To Love" which became a hit in Europe. I took Brenda to Los Angeles and stayed at Ted Tickton's home in Beverly Hills. Brenda lived with her mother nearby. Since Brenda had aspirations to be in the movies, I introduced her to my friend of long standing, Danny Simon, playwright Neil Simon's brother and himself an extremely accomplished playwright. My husband, Philip, thought that Danny's "Convertible Girl" had more substance than anything

Brenda Smith was another "Broken Dream," broken, that is, by her manipulative mother.

Danny Simon, brilliant playwright and vocal coach, helped me prepare Brenda.

Faith O'Hara, right, with Billy Sherrill, rear, producer Noro Wilson and me in Nashville.

his brother ever wrote, although it never had as much popularity as Neil's best plays.

Danny had not finished a project he began based on his own experience with an overly fastidious roommate. His brother took over the project which became a monster stage hit, then a movie known as *The Odd Couple*. Ever helpful, and an acting coach of some distinction, Danny worked with me to develop Brenda's acting skills. Together, we prepared Brenda for an audition which was carefully staged in Ted's large living room to a select group of Motion Picture people including Director Vincent Minelli, whom Danny knew well. The audition was successful and Brenda soon afterward was selected for a bit part in a production scheduled to open before the end of 1972. As soon as she was cast, her mother followed Beau Tucker's example and dropped me as her manager, taking over management chores herself. Brenda appeared in a few more movies but never, as far as I can recall, in a starring role. Properly managed, I believe Brenda might have gone much farther as a singer and, possibly, as an actress as well.

Also, late in 1972, a lady named Barbara Barber brought a beautiful, sweet-tempered blonde, Faith O'Hara, to me to help with her management. I was impressed with her singing and with her winsome ways so I took her and Barbara to Nashville. Billy Sherrill signed her to a Columbia contract and Noro Wilson produced her songs on Columbia's label. On January 29 of 1974, I was invited by the CBS convention in Atlanta, Georgia to present Faith to the four thousand assembled record executives and representatives of the record industry where she performed her new Columbia release, "Crying Steel Guitar," and five other songs. Faith was launched by Columbia in this all-out manner and remained faithful to me. She succeeded but eventually married and dropped out of sight. A highlight of the banquet for me personally was a tribute paid to me by Master of Ceremonies Ron Bledsoe, recounting what he termed my "incredible ability to find and develop talent." While the focus of the event was on Faith, I was flattered with Ron's tribute to me for finding, developing and promoting Faith, Brenda Smith, Tanya Tucker and others. I did not speak of the Tucker treason, but Ron went on at length about the way Tanya dropped Billy Sherrill and signed with MCA for more money — par for the

Billy Sherrill, center, asked me to take over Management of Vicky Fletcher, a great singer.

course, I thought — but I continued to be protective of Tanya. I was next asked by Billy Sherrill to work with a lovely Italian-American singer named Victoria Gilano Fletcher. "Vicky" was being managed by a powerful top-echelon manager with whom Billy had problems. Billy did not feel comfortable taking his orders and asked me to take over the management. Billy applied his skill as a writer to Vicky's first recording session. Vicky and I got along splendidly and we soon became close friends, as we still are today. I quickly placed her on Johnny Carson's *Tonight Show* and other highly visible appearances such as the Danny Thomas show. Subsequently, Vicky completed a successful Far East Tour and for a time it seemed that she might become an international sensation. We traveled together on tour with another old friend, the famous country singer Mickey Gilley, and Vicky soon moved near me in Las Vegas. She recorded the song that I had written for Tanya, "I Love The Way He Loves Me," again produced for Columbia Records by Billy Sherrill, and it enjoyed successful distribution — as did several other songs Vicky recorded — in particular, "Che Bella Giorno" (or "A Beautiful

Vicky and I traveled with Mickey Gilley throughout the country for a while.

Morning") in 1975. This song, also produced by Billy Sherrill for Columbia, was published by my friend Al Gallico, who publicized it as adding "a touch of old Italy to the Nashville sound," further broadening Nashville's music appeal — which had been Billy's aim from the beginning of his work at Columbia.

Vicky appeared at the Las Vegas Hilton and with Johnny Paycheck at the Landmark Hotel, Caesar's, the Dunes and the Riviera, among other Las Vegas venues. Vicky bought a home near me in Las Vegas. She began to tire of being on the road and decided to retire after her growing fame got her into trouble — a sensational episode that created headlines. Vicky was coming home one night after work when she was kidnapped at gunpoint. Two vicious thugs seized her and assured her she was headed for ". . . a hole in the desert" unless she gave them $50,000 immediately. Vicky was certain she was going to be killed even if she could find a way to come up with the money. She had to overcome her fears and out-think her captors. "The only place where I could get that kind of money is the Riviera cage," she said, "because I have a line of credit there." Fortunately, her captors took her to the Riviera, where she deliberately behaved in a way that aroused suspicion with the floor manager, who knew her well. As she passed him, she rolled her eyes back toward the two thugs following her and, in an unfriendly manner, said she had to ". . . get some money from the cage." That was the tip-off and the floor manager immediately called the security guard. The thugs were apprehended, tried, convicted and sent to prison. Vicky moved to California, eventually bought a home in Palm Springs from Priscilla Presley and, after selling it in 2005, moved back to Las Vegas where once more she resides with her loveable sister. Vickie always remained a faithful friend who again lives close by.

Returning to Ronnie Fuller: By 1974 Ronnie was appearing at the Golden Nugget Hotel and Casino where Steve Wynn presided as Entertainment Director. At the time, it was the most elegant of the Las Vegas downtown casinos — and Ronnie kept on being held over by popular demand. Steve Wynn was a close personal contact because I had been bringing talent to him and other casino managers in Las Vegas. Steve was very helpful to me and I was most appreciative of that help and profoundly regret that I no longer am close to the man that has done so much for Las Vegas. Ronnie Fuller became a close friend of Steve's, but could not shed light. I think that I blew that contact inadvertently by introducing Steve to a beautiful lady, Rodell Henshaw, who happened to be with me one day when I had an appointment with Steve. I never found out what happened but, after taking Rodell for a ride to California in his private jet, Steve stopped taking my calls. Later, my old friend, Perry Fuller — no relation — a masseur and personal fitness trainer who used to be in constant demand by Natalie Cole, Mrs. Paul Getty and top boxers (almost single-handedly, Perry's training was responsible for Joe Foreman's championship comeback) confirmed my theory after giving one of his fabulous massages to Rodell. I liked Steve and truly regretted losing his friendship. I still don't know for certain what happened.

Having unbounded faith in Ronnie, I took him to such Hollywood producers as Hal Wallis and Joe Pasternak for auditions. Their interest in signing Ronnie to a film contract was genuine, but before this next plateau could be reached, it became clear that Ronnie had a health problem and needed medical treatment. He returned home to Wisconsin and I learned through numerous telephone calls that he was under a lot of prescription medications. A tour had been scheduled featuring Ronnie that was to establish him as a sensational new entertainer capable of filling stadiums and concert halls. I had worked for many months to set up the tour, coordinating it with a planned recording session, music publishing and major publicity. Time passed. Ronnie did not return and I was forced to substitute someone else in his place. But now (2006), Ronnie is singing his songs again. Recently, in 2003, I sent Billy Sherrill a number of Ronnie's songs for him to review. Billy told me that if he had not retired and was still active in the music field, he would ". . . sign Ronnie in a heartbeat." I have always respected Billy's judgment of talent, so those words validated the confidence I've had in Ronnie all along. Only recently, I learned that Ronnie succeeded in releasing two albums in Europe that have reached the top of the charts there. Not only that, Ronnie's songs individually are *all* on the charts with rave comments from a staggering array of music reviewers worldwide. On September 20, 2005, I received a truly amazing report from Comstock Records, Ronnie's distributor in Europe, Australia and elsewhere abroad that cites the most impressive compilation of airplay comments that I have ever seen since Elvis Presley was at his zenith. "Superb voice and arrangements" (Denmark), "18 good tracks from Ronnie — what an album!" (Scotland), "Great voice and great songs — a great man" (Germany),

"Great album — many fine songs here" (Australia). Not only is Ronnie Fuller now dominating country music airplay around the world, his best-selling book, "I Will Sing My Songs Again" tells the story of his amazing life and is being made into a docu-drama for television. So Ronnie *is* singing his songs again and is being closely tracked by the Country Music Association of Europe. Ronnie now has a hundred original songs that he has written, arranged, produced and recorded by himself! More amazing is the remarkably high quality of his songs and his own voice singing them. In my opinion, Ronnie's mega-talent covers such a broad spectrum that he may very well have a permanent influence on the direction of American music as his creativity unfolds during the next five years. His songs have a compelling, haunting quality that stays in one's mind, demanding to be heard repeatedly. I recently spoke with Al Gallico who, like Billy, is now retired and regrets not having contacts in the contemporary field to get involved in the Fuller phenomenon. But Ronnie is definitely happening at long last and my confidence in his ability to get his songs to the American Public is unflagging. If he has to make his impact felt first in Europe and overseas, then so be it. That suggests coming from the outside to the inside which is opposite to the usual progression in American music. Something that Ronnie also has in abundance is intellectual integrity. He followed my saga with Tanya Tucker and remains disgusted with the lack of loyalty and integrity she showed. I do not share his feeling on this point because I witnessed first hand Tanya's relationship with her domineering father and his determination to control her career and to profit by it. Certainly that has happened so it is Beau Tucker's ethics and integrity that is the issue, not Tanya's.

Way back in 1975, Ronnie wrote a song called "We All Play The Same Guitar" which I understand became something of a hit in certain markets. The song was a memorable one and, in 1982, it was the song that gave me the idea of a Broadway-type stage musical with some minor changes in lyrics. The melody was perfect the way it was written by Ronnie, so I left it alone. Ronnie had obtained a copyright of the original version and the two of us obtained a copyright on the new version because we felt that it was important. We called this new version "Country, Soul, Rock-'n'-Roll." This new version formed the entire conceptual basis of a stage show that I put together for the Riverside Hotel and Casino in Laughlin, Nevada. In fact, it became the show's theme song, tying together different genres of guitar-based popular music, showing the interrelationship of country music, soul and rock and roll. That show was so successful in Laughlin, Nevada, that the Riverside Hotel Resort and Casino invited us back for the following year. Then, in the spring of 1983, a producer named John Stewart came to Laughlin to see the show. He was excited about it and developed a proposal for The Imperial Palace, taking the concept, but not the song that generated the concept, to The Imperial Palace Hotel and Casino on the Las Vegas Strip where he called it *Legends in Concert*. He even signed one of my principal performers, Dana McKay, an exceptionally good Elvis Presley impersonator, to a contract for performing in the show which he then produced. I had Dana under contract at the time, but I did not try to block Dana from going to the Imperial Palace because, at that point, the long daily 90-mile commute to Laughlin was beginning to tire me and I planned to discontinue the show anyway. Dana gave me a copy of his agreement with Stewart and a description of Stewart's outline-proposal to the Imperial Palace ". . . in case anything happened," as he put it. I had no idea what he meant by this, but, since I was planning to close my show at the Riverside and already was deep into plans to develop a real estate project which I called "Dolores Village," I saw no need for clarification. Some years later, Dana was murdered at his home in Las Vegas, apparently connected with some sort of drug deal, according to the "Las Vegas Review/Journal." I was fond of Dana (as was everyone) and miss his friendship. I don't know if his murder had anything to do with the documentation Dana entrusted to me when he went with John Stewart, but recently I have begun to wonder about it. Since the Dana McKay murder has not yet been solved, I have decided that it might be wise if I lay low and take a wait-and-see approach. Meanwhile, not only was *Legends in Concert* a smash success on the Vegas Strip, where it has had a continuous run for the past twenty-some years, but also the show has been franchised worldwide earning many, many millions! To this day, neither Ronnie nor I have seen a single dime from this mega-success. It remains Ronnie's intellectual property and perhaps partly mine as well because I thought of creating a show with his song. The last chapter in the **Legends in Concert** saga has yet to be written. Stay tuned.

When Ronnie's illness forced him to leave Las Vegas in the mid 1970's, he returned to his home in Wisconsin where he was improperly diagnosed and became far worse by being prescribed too many medications. That medical malpractice deprived him of many successful years of a career which had just begun to "take off" before he left Las Vegas. Thirteen years ago, in February of 1982, I prepared a notarized statement for Ronnie's malpractice lawsuit containing much of the above information and concluding as follows: "There is no doubt in my mind that the public relations momentum behind Ronnie Fuller (who, in appreciation, had professionally adopted my surname in exchange for Beasaw), and his indisputable talent would have made him a major entertainment figure had he returned to a full working schedule and the good health that this vigorous young man had shown. He was energetic, good-looking, talented, drug-free, poised, confident and very ambitious. It was devastating to me that he was unable to continue working in our profession, which rewards talent and hard work more than any other that I know." The upshot is that despite these personal health setbacks, Ronnie still stands as a talented, dedicated professional who once more is exciting audiences with his onstage charisma and song-writing power. He remains to this day a dear and valued friend whose star once again is rising, as Ronnie's distributor, Frank Fara of Comstock Records, Ltd. verified in a letter dated October 5, 2005: "It has indeed been a pleasure introducing you and your music to the international music markets. You have garnered an immense amount of compliments from DJ's around the world. Your 'Greatest Songs'/ Two-album collection made quite an impact on DJ's and programmers. It was truly amazing to have some Program Directors tell us that they would play *all* of your songs. What a feat considering you have 18 songs on each album. I believe this must truly be a first." Parallel with this extraordinary musical success, Ronnie's book "I Will Sing My Songs Again" has shot to the top of international bestseller lists, has been translated into several languages and is now sold in 45 countries. In November of 2005, Ronnie's publisher signed a contract with

Walmart, something most writers dream about and few ever achieve.

My own career went into hiding when I remarried Paul B. Sogg in 1978. That forced interruption of my professional life might be termed a "grand hesitation" similar to the one Ronnie Fuller was experiencing, though not for the same reasons. I was seduced by the illusion of "security" with Sogg, and that marriage ended, not by being savaged again by his dogs but by his almost unbelievable unfairness to my son, Darrel, who worked for nearly two years selling houses from Sogg's development on the promise that the last eight home sales in "Barry Acres" would be entirely his to keep. Instead, Sogg refused to honor his agreement (it was oral and Sam Goldwyn's dictum, "an oral agreement ain't worth the paper it's written on," again must be repeated as it certainly applies here) and Darrel saw no way to win litigation against a man who had a net worth in excess of forty million dollars. Darrel's wonderful wife, Linda, left him principally over this matter and Darrel began to drink heavily. As for myself, I had at least signed a prenuptial agreement with Sogg granting me the right to buy my choice of fifteen acres at the same low price he had paid from a one-hundred eighty-acre plot of land that I had brought to him. Not surprisingly, he charged me fifty percent more than he paid, but even this inflation, in my opinion, still made it a bargain, so I proceeded to pay him and go my own way. The attorney who handled this deal and my second divorce from Sogg was Michael Bessman, recently arrived in Las Vegas from Detroit. Mike could be every bit as charming as Sogg and, I suspect, took double pleasure in beating Sogg out of his wife and winning me at the same time. Jumping out of one bad marriage into another, even worse union, was something I cannot begin to explain. With all his legal expertise, Mike Bessman actually talked me out of leaving a meeting where I was effectively fleeced out of my land by a man who looked like a crook, spoke like a crook, acted like a crook and — yes, certainly was a crook. Mike should have protected me with his legal insight and not pressured me into signing a document that brought nothing of value to the table and only made me vulnerable to losing something I had worked many years to acquire. Could Mike have been bribed by the nefarious Dennis McGaughey? I may never know, but other

I married Paul Sogg two many times.

treacherous actions by Mike lead me to suspect that this may well have been the case.

But why had I not learned to be more discriminating in my choice of men? I had been pursued by Cliff Jones, the tall, dark and charming Lt. Governor of Nevada whom I had met in Pamplona, Spain during the "running of the bulls" — now wasn't that an appropriate occasion for a powerful bull of a man to run after me? — or was it the other way around? But Cliff had experienced as many bad choices in the women he married as I had bad choices in men and both of us were unhappily married at the time. We commiserated with one another and remained friends, not lovers. I was far more fortunate than Cliff, because I finally found Philip, whereas Cliff was cornered by a grasping, self-serving female when he was most vulnerable. Paul Sogg was after me to marry him again when a tall, handsome man I had known for many years, a former Clark County District Attorney and Judge Pro Tem, Edward G. "Ted" Marshall, began to romance me. Ted was an advisor to my

Cliff Jones, Pamplona Paramour

dear friend, Aria Allen's National Artists Foundation. He volunteered to handle my legal work and invited me to visit NORAD with him. I enjoyed Ted's company immensely and viewed him as a preferable alternative to Paul Sogg, despite Sogg's millions. Ted was a dedicated Mormon, quite high in the Mormon Hierarchy and wanted me to study the tenets of the Church of Jesus Christ of the Latter Day Saints preparatory to conversion. I wanted to learn about Mormon beliefs and went with Ted to Salt Lake City for a week of study for that purpose, but the entire question became moot with the unexpected appearance of Dr. Philip Chamberlin. I am asking that he tell here what happened in his own words because it's a wonderful, romantic story and I want him to participate in this book as we have worked together since we met:

PHILIP CHAMBERLIN: "About 1981 I was asked by my friend, Dr. Aria Allen, to join the Board of National Artists Foundation. At the time, I was trying to launch the Hollywood Museum and had left my post as Director of Special Projects at the Academy of Motion Picture Arts and Sciences to concentrate on that daunting task.

"Dr. Allen died in June of 1986 and in her will named my friend, Gene Dedlow, and me as co-executors of her estate. It fell to me to deliver her gold and platinum watch to her 'best friend' in Las Vegas. By coincidence, I was scheduled to be flown to Las Vegas to evaluate a laser projector for its manufacturer and took the watch with me. After evaluating the machine's performance, I called Dolores Fuller, and then took a taxi to her home. Dolores came to the door, a vision in pink that struck me forcefully. She looked far younger than I expected for a 'best friend' of Aria Allen who was somewhat older than I. We talked for at least three hours in her living room and discovered that we had an extraordinary number of interests in common and many shared enthusiasms. When it came time for me to leave, she offered to drive me to the airport for my return to Los Angeles. As Dolores dropped me off, she leaned over and kissed me full on the mouth. The Hollywood style is to kiss or brush cheeks, so I was somewhat astonished and did not easily recover. Come to think of it, I still have not. About two weeks later, Dolores called to say she was coming in for one of her periodic visit to Dr. Walzak and suggested we get together for a drink. I countered with an offer to pick her up at the airport. From that moment forward, I determined never to let her out of my sight. Dolores had some business in El Monte which required her to stay over and I suggested the Hollywood Roosevelt Hotel which was undergoing revitalization. It occurred to me that I, too, was experiencing revitalization.

"When I went to Fort Myers Beach, Florida, to visit my mother two months later, Dolores came down to meet her and stayed a few days. Mother commented on how nice Dolores looked in her bathing suit and was even more impressed with the way she pitched in with cooking, dishes and housework, finally giving me the verdict I had hoped for: 'She is useful as well as decorative!'

ABOVE: **Aria Allen here was much younger and an actress when she first became my friend.**

LEFT: **Ted Marshall was on Aria Allen's Advisory Board when we began dating.**

We flew back together and, 32,000 feet over Colorado, I asked Dolores if she would marry me when my ship comes in. I am still waiting for the ship, but Dolores decided to wait with me so we were married 22 months later. Mother was a bit concerned that Dolores had so many marriages that ours might not last, but I assured her that 'sometimes it is best to keep trying until you get it right.' I'm happy that Dolores kept trying and I am determined to keep trying to have her feel that, indeed, she did get it right. I know that I got it right."

Here are Philip and I in 1987 waiting for his ship to come in.

Cliff Jones divorced after I found Philip and had no use for a huge, elegant, crystal chandelier in his small apartment, so he gave it to us feeling, he said, that he didn't want to put it in storage and that it somehow seemed to have a perfect home in our dining room. Less than four years later, Cliff again married and one day came to our door unannounced with his new wife, who barged in rudely demanding to see "Cliffie's chandelier." Cliff sheepishly apologized for his surprise visit and softly asked if he could please take back the $15,000 chandelier he had "loaned" me. Philip was completely

Artist-friend Jeanne Williams cuts a fine figure on my pool deck.

against complying with this request since we had spent quite a bit reinforcing and replastering our dining room ceiling, but Cliff's badgering bride soon turned the request into a demand backed by the implied involvement of Cliff's Las Vegas law firm. I had no stomach for a court fight with my old boy friend but Philip was entirely correct in observing that Cliff's friendship had ended when he allowed himself to be pussy-whipped yet again. The chandelier went from our home straight into storage — after all, there were already three other chandeliers in his wife's home and subsequent calls to Cliff were intercepted, as was my "let's stay friends" letter which was steamed open, resealed and returned by the wife with a stamp reading "delivery refused." It was not long afterward that poor Cliff died. It seemed clear to me that his personal life was unhappy to the end. We have a new chandelier that is smaller and less elegant, but it suits us just fine. In fact, we bought a used chandelier that had been damaged and this afforded me the chance to apply my creative energy in a way that was more physical than is song writing. I found a musty old shop in Vegas that had lots of crystal and selected several dozen pieces to repair the old relic, working on my bedroom patio in front of an eight-foot by sixteen-foot bas relief that my artist friend Jeanne Williams and I had sculpted years before.

My husband, Philip, and I worked together on the restoration of Eddie's unfinished featurette, *Crossroads of Laredo*. We have always loved working together.

Ed Wood posthumously re-enters Show Biz
Chapter Fourteen

Early in 1994, my phone started ringing with the news that Touchstone Films, an independent production company under the Disney banner, was coming out with a biographical film on the period of Ed Wood's life when Eddie, Bela Lugosi and I were in Hollywood working together on low-budget movies. The first of those phone calls was from Brett Thompson, a promising young film maker who was racing to get his documentary on Eddie out in time to take advantage of the revival of interest in the man I had lived with and supported for nearly four years.

Brett Thompson and me at the shoot for his documentary film on Edward D. Wood, Jr.

Brett wanted to interview everyone who worked with Eddie, so arrangements were made for me to go down to Hollywood from Las Vegas and do an on-camera interview. Brett worked meticulously to create a set for each of seventeen surviving "Wood-workers" that would put us in environments meant to evoke our individual histories. Unfortunately for Brett, another talented young film maker, Ted Newsom, quickly put together an interview film called *Look Back In Angora* which rode the crest of a big wave of interest in Eddie generated by Rudolph Grey's superbly researched study, "Nightmare of Ecstasy: The Life and Art of Edward D. Wood, Jr." (Feral House, 1992) — used as a source by the script-writers of the forthcoming Disney release of Tim Burton's 1994 film, *Ed Wood*. This impressively edited movie rapidly became a bestseller for Rhino Home Video and featured a number of Wood "alumni," myself included. "People" magazine called me just prior to October, 1994's wide release of *Ed Wood* and arranged for their Los Angeles writer, Lois Armstrong, to come to Las Vegas for an interview (Oct. 31, 1994), followed by one of their top-notch photographers, Sam Jones, who came up from Los Angeles a few days later and shot photos for her article. When the film opened at the Galaxy Theatre in Hollywood on September 27, 1994, Disney sent a limo to take us to the premiere. The after-party was held in Musso and Frank's, a classic Hollywood restaurant and watering hole featured in the Burton film as the place where Eddie supposedly met Orson Welles and renewed his determination to make movies his own way. Sarah "Jurassic" Parker refrained from mixing with those who attended, unlike the gentlemanly Martin Landau and, instead, cloistered herself with a few of her friends in a private booth. We sought her out in a friendly approach, only to get a rude cold shoulder treatment that said, in effect, "How dare you intrude on my space!" If she didn't bother to call me before portraying my life with Eddie, why did I expect that she might be more hospitable in person? Film critics and film buffs were unanimous in their enthusiasm for the movie, although not for Parker's mannered performance. Why, then, was the box office not better? What I learned suggests that much of the explanation had to do with studio politics. Frank Wells, President of Disney (and a friend of Philip's), had been killed about a year earlier in a tragic skiing accident and it was widely expected that Jeffrey Katzenberg would succeed him at Disney. Katzenberg had persuaded Tim Burton to join Disney but, when the head of Disney, Michael D. Eisner, failed to elevate Katzenberg, Steven Spielberg and Sid Geffen made him an offer he didn't delay one single second to accept. Katzenberg joined what would become the wildly successful SKG Dreamworks Studio (subsequently acquired by Paramount) as a full partner in charge of animation and quickly proceeded to take animation leadership away from Disney or, as it is often called in Hollywood, the "Mouse House." Once Katzenberg was out the Disney door, Burton's film was dumped into wide release instead of being given the special handling that *Ed Wood* deserved. In our view, the Burton film should have been released first in a few key theatres nationwide and been given time for "word-of-mouth" to generate a much larger box office. While certainly not a box office failure, it could not be called a hit with the general film-going public. Those who were interested in film making and in film history found a way to see it — often more than once. Tim Burton promptly left Disney, which might have been the logical studio to release Burton's 2005 hits *Charlie and the Chocolate Factory* and *The Corpse Bride*. All were money-makers and all of this would seem to prove that Eisner's judgment in the choice of executives for leadership at Disney has been deeply flawed. This was confirmed by Eisner's disastrous decision to bring Michael Ovitz to Disney, followed by a compounding failure to support him. Apparently the Mouse Factory's Board of Directors came to this conclusion because Eisner retired in October of 2005 after a "no confidence" vote by Disney's Board and considerable criticism. It is ironic that ten years after throwing *Ed Wood* into wide release and, in effect, dumping Depp, Disney has virtually been saved by Johnny Depp's creation, *Pirates of the Caribbean*, a "tentpole" that has taken in more than a billion dollars for the three-part series. Johnny didn't write or direct the pirate movies, but the extraordinary way he interpreted his role — even doing his own make-up — made the movie entirely his own. Disney executives were nervous about what he was doing at first, but quickly came around once they saw the results.

Wade Williams, who has been responsible for much of the success of *Ed Wood* and the re-release of Eddie's films worldwide, invited me to appear at the opening of the film in one of his Kansas City theatres. Imagine my astonishment to get there and find my name on the theatre marquee forty years after I had left movies for song writing! Not only that, but on opening day, the "Kansas City Star" hit me with a headline, "Ed Wood Made Her A Star"! Here I had rarely even mentioned Eddie when speaking about my career and suddenly I am the focus of all this attention because of the Disney movie about my old boy friend, my dear friend Bela and myself. The story in the "Kansas City Star" was timed to coincide with the opening, so the theatre was packed, the film was enthusiastically received and, for the following discussion session, I was introduced by my husband, Philip, who chose to wear one of my angora sweaters for the occasion. In the more than ten years since then, we have had many enjoyable appearances at film festivals and celebrity autograph signings around the country that show no signs of abating. Perhaps the most important of these was the red carpet, all expenses, round-trip to the Munich International Film Festival in July of 1995 for Philip and me, co-sponsored by the Festival and Buena Vista's European office (the distribution arm of Disney). *Ed Wood* had its European premiere at the Festival along with *Glen or Glenda? Plan Nine from Outer Space*, *Bride of the Monster*, *Crossroads of Laredo* and a rough cut of Brett Thompson's *The Haunted World of Edward D. Wood, Jr.* All of these were chosen by Ulla Rapp, the festival's brilliant programmer for independent films. My job was to introduce *Ed Wood* and the other four Ed Wood movies. In turn, I was presented to the Munich audiences by the distinguished film critic and principal programmer of the San Francisco International Film Festival, Albert Johnson, who delighted in his job and insisted on performing it in my last remaining angora sweater, the very same cardigan that Eddie himself borrowed so often forty years before. I still have that sweater! I was interviewed on film for television at least twice every day which left very little time for me to see many of the festival's richly varied premieres or to socialize with the beautiful and talented actress, Theresa Russell, her husband, director Nicolas Roeg, or the legendary director, Budd Boetticher, among my fellow festival guests. During many of my moments in interviews, I noticed a beautiful tall young blonde whom I mistakenly took for one of the many actresses there. At one

RIGHT: **Regina Goetze, talented director of an excellent one-hour documentary on my life up to 1997.**

BELOW: **Beverly Garland and I were guests at Monster Bash 2000, Eddie is behind us.**

point we finally spoke and I learned that she was a film director, Regina Goetze, who had been studying me with the notion of using me for a documentary film she had in mind. This she did for German Television the following year.

Already I had attended a festival at Rutgers University as an honored guest and "Chiller Theatre," the largest of the memorabilia shows, where I met film maker Karl Petry. Karl asked both me and Philip to appear in a film he had been planning and when I came to New Jersey the following spring, he created a cameo role, that of Theresa Powell, a movie star who had an affair with *The Ironbound Vampire* some thirty years before visiting him at a party held in her honor at the vampire's mansion. She has no idea it is the same man she left for a Hollywood contract because "Mr. Lane" is very young, yet a celebrated writer. Amazingly, he greatly resembles her old flame who, of course, could not follow her to sunny California (vampires do not like the sun). There were a great many original touches in Karl's little movie. It led the new pattern of films made, not for theatrical release, but especially for video, where it set sales records and paved the way for Karl's subsequent directorial efforts. Philip, who also had a role in the film, and I studied our lines in the car on the way to the shoot, many aspects of which reminded me of the way Eddie worked forty years before.

KARL PETRY: What made my film *The Ironbound Vampire* such a success was Dolores Fuller being in the cast. When Dolores came on the set it was like royalty walked in. You must remember in the world of "B" movies Dolores Fuller is considered a goddess. This is the woman who will forever be linked with the King of cult movies, Ed Wood, Jr. Since the cast and crew are based out of the New York City area the predominate clothing color is black, this is a big plus when making a vampire movie, however this is not the case with Dolores, who sparkles with her light colored clothing laced with rhinestones and beads. Her daily attire looks like she just walked off a stage in Las Vegas. This is quite the contrast in making a vampire film. One incident stands out regarding the making of the film. One of the pitfalls of making low budget films is the fact that you are at the mercy of strangers who will allow you to use their property for a shoot. The day of the party scene the people who promised us the use their home decided not to. I had only one day to shoot with Dolores and that would have been lost without a location. I turned in a panic to Andrew T. Berry and Gita Rothschild, both prominent attorneys from a prestigious law firm in New Jersey asking them the use of their home that evening. When I mentioned to them that

Richard Matyskiel (the Vampire) welcomes Philip and me to a party at his mansion in a scene from Karl Petry's best-selling DVD *The Ironbound Vampire* (1998).

Dolores Fuller would be part of the cast coming to their home it surprised me to see that Drew Berry knew exactly who she was, permission was given immediately and the shoot went on as scheduled. This is the magic of Dolores. By the time we left not one person walked away without an autograph. Speaking of autographs, the next day she was a guest on the Comcast Network TV show called, *Family Talk*. When we arrived at the studio in Union, NJ the only person we saw was the receptionist, we announced ourselves and were let in. Lisa Spagnuolo one of the producers met us in the hall then brought us to the waiting room. Someone from somewhere must have announced that Dolores was in the building when suddenly we were surrounded by fans of workers from Comcast wanting to meet her and get their prized autograph. I will always remember this time. I am a witness to the popularity this woman still has. Being with her makes you feel like you are a star too. It's what I fondly call the magic of Dolores Fuller.

— **Karl Petry**

I also appeared in two direct-to-video productions for my old friend, Ted V. Mikels. The first was a movie made in 1998 called **Dimensions in Fear**, where I played the part of the "TV Station Owner." Then I did a cameo in **Corpse Grinders II**, which was a sequel to a popular cult film he'd made some years before. In the movie, which was shot in Las Vegas, I played Patricia Grant and have a scene as a product demonstrator in a supermarket. Actually, Philip has a larger part and does a wonderful comical turn as Mr. Yonkers, an unhinged *undertaker*!

During the mid-1990's, Brett Thompson completed his documentary feature **The Haunted World of Edward D. Wood, Jr.**, co-produced by Crawford John Thomas (nicknamed "CJ"), a West Los Angeles roofing contractor who, I was amazed to learn, had co-produced Eddie's first movie, **Crossroads of Laredo**, in 1948 when CJ was only eighteen years of age. Eddie learned that CJ had inherited a small amount of money and talked him into forming a film production company. CJ told me that he still had the footage for Eddie's first film which had never been finished or even assembled in a way that would be suitable for showing as a work print. Furthermore, the sound track, if there ever was one, had been lost. CJ asked Philip and me if we could do anything with the material, considering the 1990's surge of interest in Eddie. We looked at a poor video copy of the 16mm film and found it so interesting that we decided to see what could be done. And so it was that after a hiatus of forty years, I found myself once again working with Eddie!

Eddie and CJ had only about two thousand dollars for their production, but it didn't take long for Eddie to come up with the story outline. He found it in the lyrics to the old "Cowboy's Lament," also known as "The Streets of Laredo." Eddie was fond of the song and it did tell a story. CJ was swept up by Eddie's enthusiasm and went along with the idea of using the song for a story line as well as for the title and sound track theme of their movie. They quickly decided to shoot the film at a ranch in Saugus, California — about fifty miles from Hollywood — that provided a suitable "Western" feeling for Laredo which neither Eddie nor CJ had ever visited, being off the beaten track on the southern border of Texas. Eddie was a great enthusiast for low-budget western movies as well as "B" movies of all kinds and his choice of location still seems right today, perhaps because a great many westerns were shot in that general area and shared a common geographical feeling. Eddie also selected Ruth McCabe, a lovely, slim actress as the leading lady and Duke Moore as the leading man. He used Moore on several of his subsequent films as well as Don Nagel, who played the anti-hero. Eddie hired veteran Hollywood cameraman, Ray Flin, to handle the 16mm camera. All of his cast and crew were paid union scale, including CJ, who took the part of a sheriff's deputy. This meant, of course, that CJ was paid with his own money — which hardly mattered since CJ later had to put it back into the production in order to continue. Eddie tried to finish the film in a single day's shooting, but travel time to Saugus made it impossible, so a second day's filming was scheduled later at a location near the Hollywood Bowl. On this second day, Eddie himself handled the camera, but did not follow the "Streets of Laredo" lyrics precisely — perhaps because trade papers had begun to write about a forthcoming Paramount production called *Streets of Laredo* to star William Holden, Macdonald Carey and William Bendix that in fact was released the following year. A great many film projects announced with great fanfare never materialize, but this one did. In any event, the reality of a major Hollywood production supported by public familiarity with a traditional song of the same title killed any chance a small independent film maker with no previous experience might have had to raise money. The Paramount film sadly ended the ambitions of Wood/Thomas Productions. Eddie was soon pursuing other interests, leaving CJ with a few cans of useless footage. Forty-six years later, another major Hollywood studio is shooting a film about Edward D. Wood, Jr. and it was then that CJ approached us. My husband, Philip, who had produced several films, restored several others and is something of an authority on the history of film, undertook to do a shot analysis of *Crossroads* and found that Eddie used one hundred thirty different camera set-ups in the course of only twenty-two minutes of film. As we studied Eddie's first little film, our respect for his talent kept growing, despite several sequences that might be termed stereotypical Wood touches, such as placing the camera on the wrong side of the horses as the cowboy (played by Eddie) is overtaken and killed by Don Nagel just as the film is beginning. Later, when Don Nagel awkwardly mounts his horse and nearly falls off as he hastily rides out of sight, it is clear that neither Eddie nor Don had experience riding horses — however many horse operas they may have seen. Two of the camera pans are much too fast and, as the Parson begins his graveside service, he forgets to remove his hat. In that sequence, one can almost hear Eddie off-camera, frantically admonishing him to take it off, so he removes it and flings it aside, continuing his burial sermon without skipping a beat, but obviously skipping a much needed re-take. As in **Glen or Glenda?**, shortage of time and money made it prudent to omit additional takes. Similarly, when the song lyrics specify that his "coffin was carried by six strong young cowboys," we see only four, probably because the cardboard boxes that Eddie hastily put together to pass as a coffin were too short for six to crowd around and carry and, anyway, Eddie likely could not afford the two additional extras. In 1948, subjective camera was rarely employed, but there it is, showing the anti-hero's perspective as he turned his horse around and heads back to town. I soon came to the conclusion that the song "Streets of Laredo" needed to be rewritten so as to fit the action depicted on the screen. In fact, **Crossroads of Laredo** needed another song interpreting the action depicted, a sound track and a narration to make sense. Philip hadn't written music since the 'forties, but he saw that even "Streets of Laredo" needed to be expanded so he sat down and wrote a release to the old song which has only an eight-measure melody repeated over and over. His additional eight measures of new music and lyrics provided nice contrast, added variety and described one sequence with the Parson that everyone who has heard it loves and remembers.

For further western authenticity, I called my old friend Cliffie Stone, of country music fame, to see if he would record a narration that Philip and I had written to fill in the gaps. He agreed to do it as a favor, so Philip and I drove with Bob Evans and his Nagra tape recorder to Cliffie's home in Sand Canyon near Nuhall and worked with Cliffie to get the western flavor I had in mind. We were delighted with the result and look upon it as a tribute to dear Cliffie who had many other tributes in his lifetime, including *two* stars on the Hollywood Walk of Fame. Cliffie has since gone to that

"CJ" introduces me on film at the beginning of his and Ed Wood's little movie, *Crossroads of Laredo*, beginning its theatrical run 48 years after it was shot. Philip and I finished it.

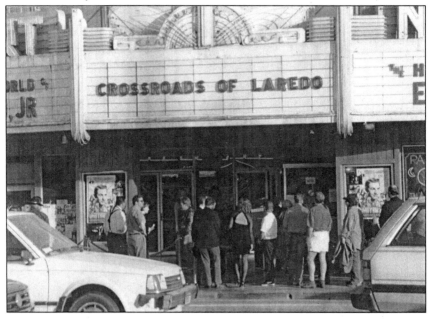

Great Broadcasting Source in the Sky, as has Bob Evans, so their work on **Crossroads of Laredo** is something of a final memorial that marks their passing. Next, I got a musician friend, Jerry Marcellino, to help me with a complete score which utilized western saloon music with honky-tonk piano, guitar, harmonica, country fiddle and drums.

All of these musicians had to be paid scale, but we had the pick of the top talent pool in Las Vegas which resulted in a cost of about ten thousand dollars, much more than the original cost of the film, even considering what a 1948 dollar would buy. I was lucky to persuade as a music collaborator, Ben Weisman, my long-time friend and co-writer for Elvis Presley, on a theme song that we thought should open the film where Eddie, as the shooting victim, rides into town and provides the motive for action that rapidly unfolds. The **Crossroads** theme has lines I intended as an elegy or final salute to my old flame: "The dreams that he carried were hardly begun; the songs in his heart remain there unsung." Both songs were sung by Elvis Aaron Presley, Jr., whom I had been co-managing for several years with Seymour Heller. "Jr.," as he is known, was brought to me by a friend, Lela Osborn, and he showed me a copy of his birth certificate to remove any skepticism I might have about his story of how his mother gave him up for adoption to Yugoslav-American parents performing with Circus Vargas. Allegedly, his mother was Dolores Hart who had an affair with Elvis during the late 1950's and was pressured by Col. Parker to have an abortion. Being a good Catholic girl, she refused, ran away and joined Circus Vargas to hide from the Colonel and, after giving up Jr. on the condition that his adopting parents not tell him about his true lineage until he turned twenty–one, joined a Convent in Connecticut where she ultimately became a Mother Superior. Thus Junior's reluctance to speak publicly about his "Mother" so as not to embarrass her. An unauthorized book detailing Junior's astonishing story about being the illegitimate son of Elvis Presley was published in Canada and a sensationalized account then appeared in one of the scandal sheets that clutter every supermarket check-out stand. Not surprisingly, the article included a strong denial from Mother Dolores Hart. Junior was challenged, refused to submit to a DNA test and, at that point, his story changed to name as his mother an obscure Las Vegas showgirl, now deceased. I rather liked his original account, but liked his wonderful voice even more and had him record my two *Crossroads* songs. They remain to help interpret the visuals in Eddie's long lost first film. Remarkably, my rewrite of "Streets of Laredo," now called "Dust of Laredo," together with my theme-song "Crossroads of Laredo," won for me a Special Award in 1998 from ASCAP (the American Society of Composers, Authors and Publishers) — something my Elvis songs never accomplished. To qualify for the Award, songs had to be in a film production having a theatrical run within the continental United States of not less than seven days. My songs qualified because on May 1, 1996, *Crossroads of Laredo* opened at the Nuart Theatre in West Los Angeles and was featured on the theatre's marquee together with Brett Thompson's feature documentary, *The Haunted World of Edward D. Wood, Jr.* Opening night was attended by Samuel Goldwyn and his wife, Peggy, Ann Robinson (star of *War of the Worlds*), Ed Wood's daughter, Maila Nurmi ("Vampira"), and several of Eddie's "alumni." One particularly happy outcome of this auspicious opening was the attendance of C.J. Thomas's father who had, since 1948 bewailed what he considered a "stupid waste of money" by CJ in a film production that no one had ever seen. The father was incredulous and overwhelmed by the success of the opening and by Kevin Thomas's appreciative review in the "Los Angeles Times" referring to *Crossroads* as ". . . a vignette about a wayward cowboy who gets his comeuppance, and is actually more cogent than much of what was to come [from Eddie]." All was forgiven and CJ enjoyed a sweet reconciliation with his father before dying only two years later. This program established something of a box office record for documentaries, leading to repeat bookings in San Francisco, New York, Boston, Chicago and, again in Los Angeles at the Beverly Cineplex.

Regina Goetze flew in for the Los Angeles premiere to do some preliminary filming, then returned in July with a German crew that followed me around Las Vegas and tracked my husband and me to Los Angeles where she filmed Ben Weisman and me discussing the Elvis songs we wrote together. Additionally, she shot Seymour Heller and me dangling our feet in Seymour's swimming pool while

Cliffie Stone narrates *Crossroads* of Laredo in classic western style.

he told of his vain attempts to persuade Tanya and her father to stay loyal to me and to honor their contractual obligations. Tanya's rendition of "I Love The Way He Loves Me" is on the sound track of that hour-long documentary, as is one of Johnny Rivers' songs that I recorded on my own label in 1958. Excerpts from eight Elvis Presley movies featuring my songs are also included. The hour-long documentary was shown on German television in 1997. It was called ***Diamonds in the Rough*** to fit the film's theme that my life has often been dedicated to finding precious unpolished talent and developing that talent — polishing it up, if you will. Good reception led to repeat broadcasts and I obtained copies for showing here. Strong interest in an "Edward D. Wood Special" for television awaits our completion of image enhancement of the ***Crossroads*** visuals owing to nearly fifty years of neglect suffered by the original work print. When Philip and I were married in August of 1988, my close friend and former partner, Hank Levine, came to Las Vegas from Nashville and arranged our song, the Gershwin classic, "Our

Love Is Here To Stay" for the five-piece band that performed for our guests. Another of my dear Nashville friends, Sherry Mathews, sang our song which, alas! I failed to record. It would have made a beautiful memento. But then, this wonderful occasion was replete with missed opportunities: no recordings of Ben Weisman's rendering of his "Elvis Concerto" (incorporating an enhanced amalgamation of many of his fifty-seven Elvis songs); Lenny Weinstein playing a song we wrote for Tanya — sent twice to her in an expensively mounted demo with the powerful voice of lovely Tammy Graham backed by seven top Vegas musicians — but never acknowledged. (I believe that it, too, was intercepted by her father); Dexter Grey's astounding rendition of Chopin's "Polonaise" on my Steinway; a memorable soprano solo of "The Lord's Prayer"; a botched video of the ceremony and not a single decent photograph of Philip and me together. Sam Goldwyn and his wife were not able to attend, but Sam sent a heartfelt congratulatory telegram with the lovely tribute, ". . . without you, Dee, there would be no Sam and Peggy Goldwyn," an acknowledgement of their own marriage which followed the dinner party I arranged to introduce them some twenty-four years earlier. After our marriage, Philip and I left for our honeymoon that for the first week was curiously scheduled to take place at Dartmouth College in New Hampshire where Philip had a long-standing obligation to participate in the centennial conference on the life and thought of Eugene Rosenstock-Huessy. Philip's correspondence with Dr. Richard Feringer on Huessy's futuristic "Philosophy of Speech and Time" provided required reading for the opening discussion-session of this international conference with participants from 32 countries. (So of course he had to attend!) During that third week of August, New England experienced one of the hottest, most humid periods in years. We were sleeping in an ancient dormitory on lumpy cots in a room over the dorm water heaters with no air conditioning. We scoured the area trying to buy a small air conditioning unit but nothing, not even an electric fan was to be found. Such unsurpassed discomfort led us to the conclusion that if our marriage could survive the honeymoon, then the marriage itself should survive. We are now in our 22nd year together and still in love. We love working together and playing together and know that we'll always be together.

Mark Statler and me at "Monster Bash 2005." On these occasions, I met with my fans.

The second week of our honeymoon with a car generously provided by Philip's former partner, Christien Ducker, saw us in his ancestral homeland of Northern Maine (he was born in Fort Fairfield on the border of New Brunswick, Canada). We visited his sisters, I picked potatoes, then drove to Mount Desert Island on the spectacular Maine coast. There we visited with Della Perkins, Philip's cousin, with whom he lived from the fall of 1937 to the summer of 1939 while attending Pemetic Junior High School. Of course we dined on lobster, tramped through his old haunts, climbed Beech Cliff which drops precipitously into Eagle Lake and I suffered from a bad case of vertigo. Dizzy, dizzy, dizzy — or was that just the romantic part of a honeymoon finally begun? From the coast of Maine, we drove to Westboro, Massachusetts to see if the Red Barn Theatre was still there. It was not, but we spoke with a U.S. Mail carrier who remembered "the old days" of the Red Barn vividly — though not my performances of more than thirty

Howard Keel and me in July of 2004 at the show "Starstruck in Las Vegas."

years before. Oh, well. It's motion pictures that live on, not the intoxicating transience of theatre. Our next stop on our Honeymoon was New York where we dined with old friends Valerie and "Hobe" Hoberman whom I had introduced more than twenty-five years before and who where still married. We dropped by my old penthouse and found it still occupied by the lady to whom I had sold it when I left New York and returned to Hollywood a quarter-century before. Back in Las Vegas, Philip and I worked hard to save my sixteen acres of land, but in this we were unsuccessful, probably because the encumbrances made it less viable as an investment venture.

Epilogue

There still remains much to be done. My projected stage musical *Ed Wood . . . But I Wouldn't* is a project dear to my heart and is, as of this writing, about 90% completed. The death in November, 2004 of my friend, the great actor-singer, Howard Keel, dealt me a double-blow: first, the loss of yet another friend and second, still another delay of my project because Howard, a robust 84, was seriously considering my entreaty that he commit to playing Bela Lugosi on stage and I was beginning to re-tailor my script and add another song to take advantage of his titanic talent. I haven't yet given up my dreams of what I hope to accomplish with my life. What will it take to get my stage show produced? If Johnny Depp is now at the point where he can decide what to do with his life and takes an interest in my music, my show will go on. He sings in his new film and he is very good. His first love was music and I think it possible that he will broaden his scope beyond movies at some point down the road. Who knows? I'm not certain because I cannot tell when the final curtain will come down. My health has been declining lately. My husband and I were in a roll-over accident in a friend's car. Philip suffered a broken neck, a shear-fracture which only two percent survive and I received deep puncture wounds to my legs that refused to heal. Gangrene set in and did not respond to antibiotics. Three Las Vegas surgeons wanted to amputate and I knew there had to be an alternative. There was. A friend, Les Nachman, sent Dr. John Voorhees, a Naturepath, who devised two knee-high tanks into which I alternated soaking my poor legs, first in ice water, then 120 degree hot water, as long as I could bear it in each — usually two minutes — for 45 minutes each session. This stimulated the circulation and within a week, reversed the gangrene. My legs then soon healed. There are "givers" in this world and there are "takers." Mostly there are takers. Dr. John is one of the most giving people we have ever met and is remarkably intuitive in medical diagnosis and a host of other fields. He is an extraordinarily talented man and we are privileged to be counted among his inner family of friends. The motion picture field is one of the interests we have in common and John not only knows the history of movies and television, he has an exceptional memory that embraces a seemingly infinite number of details in so many areas and remembers things I have long forgotten, even about myself. More importantly, John puts these details in a meaningful context which takes them far beyond the masses of mere trivia which infect so much of our lives. Though we may have suffered financial misfortune, my husband and I are truly rich because we have friends like John.

In June of 2005, I attended the annual "Monster Bash" near Pittsburgh, Pennsylvania where I was a guest of honor for the second time in five years. Hosted by Ron and Ursula Adams, this specialized festival and celebrity event is perhaps the best organized and most professionally run get-together of its kind. As before, my husband and I had an absolutely marvelous time, but it was exhausting and the trip took so much out of me that I could hardly get out of bed for several days after returning.

Getting old is no fun, but every age has its advantages and I am blessed in many ways. I have an invention that I have used privately now for fourteen years. Those who have seen my prototype in action tell me that it should be on the market, so I am now developing that possibility. As to regaining and maintaining my health, stem cell research is going forward and inevitably will overcome obstacles thrown up by religious and political narrow-mindedness, dogma and vested interest. A new product has emerged from alternative medicine which greatly stimulates the increased production of stem cells in our own bodies. Both my legs and my heart stand to benefit from this new discovery. Science constantly amazes us as it pushes back boundaries that bind and restrict us. Every time is does, so it seems, something arises to block progress. But we live in the information age and such set-backs are only temporary. We live and learn. And we learn in order to live — and to enjoy fuller lives.

Index

Printed in the United States
142920LV00004B/11/P